Changing Doctoral Degrees

SRHE and Open University Press Imprint

General Editor: Heather Eggins

Changing
Doctoral
Degrees

An International Perspective

Keith Allan Noble

The Society for Research into Higher Education
& Open University Press

Published by SRHE and
Open University Press
Celtic Court
22 Ballmoor
Buckingham
MK18 1XW

and

1900 Frost Road, Suite 101
Bristol, PA 19007, USA

First Published 1994

A catalogue record of this book is available from the British Library

ISBN 0 335 19213 0 (hbk)

Library of Congress Cataloging-in-Publication Data

Noble, Keith Allan, 1951–
    Changing doctoral degrees: an international perspective/by
Keith Allan Noble.
        p.   cm.
    Includes bibliographical references (p.   ) and index.
    ISBN 0–335–19213–0
    1. Universities and colleges – Graduate work.   2. Degrees,
Academic.   I. Title.
LB2371.N63   1994
378.2'4 – dc20   93–14603
                                                                 CIP

Typeset by Type Study, Scarborough
Printed in Great Britain by St Edmundsbury Press, Bury St Edmunds, Suffolk

The price of doing the same old thing is
far higher than the price of change.
William J. Clinton
42nd President
United States of America

Contents

Foreword

Higher education, its cost, productivity and efficiency, are increasingly being scrutinized by governments and the public. Questions of quality assurance and accountability rivet the attention of administrators and scholars concerned with postsecondary education. Systems of accreditation and strategies for establishing degree equivalence are critical topics. But relatively little is understood of the culture of higher education. This volume provides insight into one of the most important aspects of higher education, its gatekeeper, the doctoral degree. The author has researched the available documentation to provide a history of the degree which should prove useful to scholars of higher education.

More critical to higher education decision makers, the book provides a perspective on the major characteristics of the PhD degree, and problematic issues which have been identified internationally with it. The recommendations made in this volume may perturb some, particularly in the information era. The first is that fewer students should be accepted into doctoral programmes, and the recommendations which follow present greater challenges to the university. The themes presented, however, merit critical examination, and should stimulate further discussion about the doctoral degree.

Janet G. Donald, PhD
Professor of Education
Director, Centre for University Teaching and Learning
McGill University, Montreal, Canada

Introduction

You will find this work relevant if you are an academic who advises, directs or supervises doctoral students, if you are a higher education administrator or policy maker, or if you are or will be studying for a doctoral degree. Here a doctoral degree is defined as *an academic university qualification that requires a research thesis above the master degree level*. Note this definition does not include the basic medical degree held by physicians; but it does include the medical science doctorate, based on original research and a thesis or published work, conferred after the basic medical degree or its equivalent.

Doctoral degrees have been part of higher education ever since the first was conferred in Paris *circa* 1150. Over the centuries this academic award has developed to the extent that at one time in the United States only those institutions that granted doctorates were deemed universities.

It is remarkable that this degree has survived and thrived for over eight centuries without any significant changes occurring in the acquisition process. Essentially, the same process, which was conceived and propagated in Europe and later spread first to North America then around the world, continues unchanged today.

Only in the last few decades have major adjustments to the doctoral degree acquisition process been proposed. These changes would break with long-established precedent, and consequently they do not appeal to all. Whether a change in the acquisition process will cure what is alleged to ail doctoral programmes is difficult to say. But what is not difficult to assess is that the process has considerable inertia, and any changes to the process must not be radical if they are to be adopted and accepted within traditional universities.

One issue that is most significant, and which is rarely raised during discussions about amendments to doctoral degree programmes, is the practice of granting equivalency. This practice is extremely valuable, because reciprocity is the passe-partout that opens doors to international appointments and international research opportunities. Those who hold a doctoral degree from a reputable university in one country can be offered an appointment in another country, based in part on academic reciprocity.

A doctorate provides a measure, albeit small, of an individual's intellectual weight and academic experience. This measurement, and the resultant reciprocity it allows, is possible because almost all doctoral degrees have had a similar acquisition process; exceptions include the honorary doctorates issued by many universities and the French Doctorate d'Etat.

But if radical amendments to the process are exercised, what becomes of reciprocity? What becomes of the doctoral degree as an academic passport? How will universities monitor amendments to the acquisition process implemented around the globe?

Of late, there has been an increase in the academic and public literature describing weaknesses in doctoral programmes, particularly the programme for the doctor of philosophy degree. Numerous writers have pointed out problems and possibilities for improvement, much of which could be accurate based on the high frequency and wide distribution of this literature.

Some of these recommended amendments to the doctoral degree acquisition process seem warranted and a number of them are discussed in this work. However, for traditional institutions of higher education the full force of the inertia inherent within the doctoral degree acquisition process is inescapable. And this inertia may preclude the successful adoption and/or acceptance of any significant amendments to existing doctoral programmes.

National and international inconsistencies in the use of the words dissertation and thesis exist; both words are used to describe doctoral and master-level work. For this book, however, the word thesis was selected. In addition, 'university' subsumes college, institute, school and all other places where doctoral programmes are offered. In some countries, there are lower and higher doctoral degrees. This work addresses the former, the doctorate commonly, but certainly not always, undertaken for the purpose of gaining employment in an academic or research institution. Note that individuals can, and do, attain the lower doctorate purely out of interest and are not necessarily employed in academe or in their field of study. The higher doctorate is an academic award granted for prodigious research and scholarly accomplishments over a lengthy period.

Where appropriate, additional useful information is included in the form of seven appendices. These appendices provide the reader with further information on the history, contemporary problems and current beliefs and developments with respect to doctoral degrees and there acquisition. All of these appendices have an international scope or application.

The research data in this book come from a doctoral thesis for which Professor Robert R. O'Reilly, University of Calgary, was the adviser. The book has been improved through suggestions from Dr Malcolm Tight, University of Warwick, who also drew attention to important doctoral degree practices and publications in Britain; and through the much appreciated positive criticism of three anonymous reviewers. Of course, full responsibility for the final work lies with the author.

The research results presented herein have been drawn from a study that involved 67 scholars from four English-speaking countries (Australia, Britain, Canada and the United States). Accordingly, readers need to take an international perspective when reading this work, as it was with this perspective that the book was written.

To conclude, it is hoped that this work will help reduce the tragic incidence of 'all but' former doctoral candidates; those worthy individuals who never obtained a doctorate, although they met all the requirements for the degree, but unfortunately did not complete the thesis component.

1

European Origin

Life can only be understood backwards; but it must be lived forwards.

(Kierkegaard)

The doctoral degree is old. For any study of this degree it is essential to have an historical appreciation of the university, because at one time the definition of this institution was based on the doctoral degree.

Storr (1973: 45) has drawn from Berelson's (1960) landmark study of graduate education to show that early in this century the Association of American Universities recorded, '. . . what defined a university was the offering of graduate work, and that what completed it, in essence as well as in time, was the granting of PhD degrees.' More recently, this has been reaffirmed by Rosovsky (1990: 137).

Therefore, to ensure the doctoral degree is not reviewed in isolation, an historical overview of the university is an important prologue if the European origin of the doctoral degree is to be understood. But first, a caveat is offered with respect to dates, locations and names. History succumbs to age and falters in its sureness – different sources can and do give dissimilar data.

Conception

Through a volume of collected works, Neilson and Gaffield (1986) address the perceived crisis in the contemporary university. The subtitle of their book, *A Mediaeval Institution in the Twenty-first Century*, is telling. It describes the historical period when the institution was conceived and makes the point that the concept of university as it existed in medieval times is being transferred into the twenty-first century.

It is generally accepted that the university as we know it was conceived during the Middle Ages – that period in European history between Antiquity and the Renaissance, dated from AD 476, when Romulus

Augustulus, the last emperor of the Western Roman Empire, was deposed, to AD 1453, when Constantinople was conquered by the Turks.

McNeal, Hodysh and Konrad (1981: C11) suggest that, '(i)t might be argued that the roots of the university were established in ancient Greece. Among the figures of this earlier period who contributed to the idea of higher education were Socrates, Plato and Aristotle.' Although Plato (427?–347 BC) pursued his idea of an academy for philosophic discourse on justice and virtue (Shores, 1961: 42), and the '. . . Pythagorean school of Crotona, as far back as 520 BC, had offered a variety of courses to a united scholastic community . . .' (Durant, 1939: 511), the university as it exists in Western society today arose in medieval times.

At first the collective term *studium* or *studium generale* was used, as Latin was the language of academe. Coulton (1913: 651) cites a source that has traced these terms back to 1233. Over time, the institution that took shape began to be called a *universitas*, which described one single body of students and academics.

Two higher education institutions that rose to prominence in the Middle Ages were situated at Bologna and Paris. Rashdall (1895, 1936: 19, 146, 292) identifies these institutions as the original universities, with the university at Bologna forming around 1158, and the university at Paris sometime between 1150 and 1170. Although a school of medicine did exist at Salerno, Coulton (1913: 651) dismisses this in a footnote, saying early in the eleventh century a *studium generale* did exist there '. . . but it possessed no universitatem beyond a body of Masters, of whose organization very little is known, and whose degree-giving powers were for the most part usurped by the state authorities.'

Slowly, the university concept spread across Europe. Coulton (ibid.: 654) indicates the new institutions were modelled on Bologna or Paris, although Ben-David (1977: 23, 75) believes a third archetype (Oxbridge) developed later at Oxford and Cambridge universities. Some of the earlier institutions were established *circa* as follows: 1167 Oxford, in what we now call England; 1212 Palencia, Spain; 1224 Naples, Italy; 1290 Coimbra, Portugal; 1347 Cologne, Germany; 1348 Prague, Czech Republic; 1364 Cracow, Poland; 1365 Vienna, Austria; 1411 St Andrews, Scotland; 1425 Louvain, Belgium; 1459 Basel, Switzerland; 1572 Leiden, Netherlands.

Universities revealed the existence of national and international students, who throughout Europe were seeking to expand their intellectual horizon. By the '. . . fifteenth century the university was a recognized institution with a concern for its autonomy *vis-à-vis* papal interference, with a supranational character and with concerns, customs and ceremonies . . . recognizable in the twentieth-century institutions' (Leinster-Mackay, 1977: 28, 29).

As an indication of the magnitude of these developments there were 10,000 university students in Bologna at the beginning of the thirteenth century (Chambers, 1950: 570), and the university at Paris was estimated to have had 30,000 students in 1287 (Durant, 1950:926). By the early sixteenth century there were 79 universities in Europe (Coulton, 1913:657).

Certainly the most significant change to take place after the universities were established throughout Europe was brought about by Wilhelm von Humboldt (1767–1835), the Prussian philologian and educational reformer. His officially sanctioned action altered for ever the classical concept of a university.

Humboldt's ideal was the research university, an institution where the creation of knowledge was as important as teaching in the traditional universities. The stimulus for this development stemmed from Napoleon's military defeat of Prussia in 1806. Smarting over their loss of the university at Halle, which was situated in territory forfeited to Napoleon, a new system of higher education was formulated to assist the rebuilding of the demoralized Prussian state.

This task of modernizing the older universities and the creation of new universities was assigned to Humboldt. Through his efforts as minister of education, a university was established at Berlin in 1810–12, the primary objective of which was to create knowledge. Although research at that time was commonly undertaken by the individual professor, usually in a private research academy, Humboldt brought the two concepts of teaching and research together within the single institution.

A translation of Humboldt's writing reads, '(i)f the university is restricted to the teaching and dissemination of knowledge, while the academy is assigned its advancement, one obviously does the university an injustice' (Hutchins and Adler, 1969:353). To staff the university at Berlin, '. . . professors were chosen not so much for their ability to teach, as for their reputation or willingness for original research in science or scholarship' (Durant and Durant, 1975:607).

This focus on original research was not new. Over a century earlier the university at Halle, established in 1694, was the first institution to place emphasis on creating knowledge: '. . . it vowed itself to freedom of thought and teaching, and required no pledge of religious orthodoxy from its faculty; it made room for science and modern philosophy; and, it became a centre of original scholarship and a workshop of scientific research' (ibid.:606).

One prominent intellectual founder of the university at Halle was Christian Thomasius (1655–1728). His use of German, and to a lesser extent Gottfried Wilhelm Leibnitz's (1646–1716) use of French, commenced the abandoning of Latin as the language of academe. Thomasius worked towards breaking the caste-like culture of the older professorial class, and he succeeded in '. . . bringing science and the universities into the closest connection with the actualities of life, of filling the minds of students with enlightened ideas and useful knowledge in place of the old petrified erudition' (Paulsen, 1908:118).

What Humboldt did was take the example set by Thomasius at Halle, and initiate and legislate research as a major purpose of modern universities in Prussia. Humboldt's success made Prussian universities regnant institutions that other nations envied and emulated.

In these new institutions the teaching of students was considered important, but it was no longer the primary purpose. In a translation of Humboldt's own words, '(t)he teacher no longer serves the purposes of the student. Instead both serve learning itself' (Hutchins and Adler, 1969: 350). Not every student attained a doctorate from a Prussian university however, there were also lesser qualifications, such as the Staatsexamen. This contrasts with medieval universities where Master or Doctor were the only certified qualifications granted (Simpson, 1983: 5).

Understandably, universities that were established in North America and in the former colonies of European nations were founded with the same attitudes, beliefs and customs as European institutions. Many, if not most of the senior university staff were educated in European universities (Rosenhaupt and Pinch, 1971: 118), and it was only natural that the ideas and initiatives they brought to their positions were influenced by academic traditions and values acquired in Europe. Johns Hopkins is a good example. The first predominantly graduate university in North America, Johns Hopkins '. . . had so many German-trained professors that it was referred to as "Göttingen-in-Baltimore"' (Hutchins and Adler, 1969: 346). This institution subsequently developed a world-renowned research reputation that continues to this day.

Doctor of Law, Medicine and Theology

Encel (1965: 7) mentions a Han Chinese literary examination system promulgated in 165 BC, and State examinations for public office in China commenced in 140–87 BC according to Durant (1935: 699, 700). Green (1977: 1230) claims however the formal certification of graduates on a continuous basis dates from the ninth and tenth centuries – 'Al-Azhar (established in AD 970) in Egypt and al-Qarawiyin (founded in AD 859) in Morocco awarded the *ijazah*, which was a licence or diploma. Without the *ijazah*, no scholar could practice his profession.'

Although this qualification cannot be equated directly with the doctoral degree, it represents the earliest form of qualification granted on a continuous basis. Certainly it is the forerunner of the qualifications now granted by universities in the Western world.

The date, but not the place, that the title of doctor was first conferred is disputed. Monroe (1911: 352) states that an honorary qualification was granted to Peter the Lombard and Gilbert de la Porrée in Paris in 1145. Green (1977: 1230) records that the earliest doctorate, possibly in theology, was granted after 1150 however, and Coulton (1913: 655) claims the first graduation, possibly in canon law, was that of John de Cella in about 1175.

Regardless, it suffices to say the doctor concept appears to have arisen first at the university in Paris *circa* 1150.

At Bologna, a doctorate, possibly in civil law, was conferred sometime after 1158, when the university was granted a charter by Frederick I (1123?–90, Holy Roman Emperor 1152–90). Because of this charter '. . . all graduates of Bologna could teach or practice their specialization without further examination' (Green, 1977: 1230). This doctorate was a permanent licence that was recognized and honoured by most institutions. According to Monroe (1911: 352), the jurists at Bologna attempted to arrogate the title of doctor but failed in their endeavours.

Eventually, the doctorates of law, medicine and theology were adopted at universities across the Continent. Over time the process of acquiring a doctoral degree became structured and candidates were required to complete a clearly defined and demanding academic process:

> Toward the middle of the thirteenth century the custom arose of requiring the student, after five years of resident study, to pass a preliminary examination by a committee of his nation. This involved first a private test – a *responsio* to questions; second, a public disputation in which the candidate defended one or more theses against challengers, and concluded with a summation of the results – *determinatio*. Those who passed preliminary trials were called *baccalarii*, bachelors, and were allowed to serve a master as assistant teacher or 'cursory' lecturer. The bachelor might continue his resident studies for three years more; then, if his master thought him fit for the ordeal, he was presented to examiners appointed by the chancellor . . . if the student passed this public and final examination he became a master or doctor, and automatically received an ecclesiastically sanctioned license, to teach anywhere in Christendom. As a bachelor he had taught with an uncovered head; now he was crowned with a biretta, received a kiss and a blessing from his master, and, seated in the magisterial chair, gave an inaugural lecture or held an inaugural disputation; this was his *inceptio* . . . by these and other ceremonies he was received into the magisterial guild.
>
> Durant, 1950: 929

Both Coulton (1913: 652) and Rait (1912: 16) state doctor (Latin *docere*, to teach), professor (Latin *profiteri*, to declare publicly), and master (Latin *majister*, someone greater) were used synonymously in medieval times. But Green (1977: 1230, 1231) adds, '. . . the graduates of the lower faculties (arts, grammar) were generally called master, while those of the higher faculties, (law, medicine, theology) were given the title of doctor.' Spurr (1970: 10) writes, '(a)t Paris and later at Oxford, master was the prevailing rank although the term professor was frequently used,' but '(a)t Bologna the common title was doctor, a usage that slowly spread throughout Italy and into Germany.'

The current academic usage of the word doctor stems from the early universities in Italy where the students exercised control, unlike the institutions in France where the academics were in control. Students in the Italian universities abolished doctoral prerogatives and the appellation came not to represent an office but merely an honorary title, which subsequently was transformed into an earned degree. Whereas professor, according to Spurr (1970: 10), '. . . has consistently remained a title and has come to signify universally senior rank as a teacher.' Today the usage and meaning of the words professor and doctor remain the same.

There should be no doubt that customs differed from century to century, country to country, university to university, and most probably from professor to professor. The doctorate provided evidence, as it was certified in written form authenticated with the seal of the awarding institution, that the bearer had attained all the rights and privileges attributable to that level of achievement. It allowed the holder to teach at a university, although Coulton (1913: 653) points out that a distinction existed between the teaching doctors (*legentes*) and those who obtained a doctorate but did not teach (*non-legentes*). It also enabled the bearer to teach at other institutions considered to be universities, although not all, because some institutions insisted the bearer of an external doctorate first take another qualifying examination (ibid.: 656, 657); reciprocity was not universal.

In a very practical sense the doctorate provided the holder with a means of deriving an income. A papal bull of 1292 delivered by Nicholas IV (1227–92) raised the university to new heights as an institution, and exalted the doctors at Bologna to a level of social prestige previously reserved for priests and knights (ibid.: 654). He conferred on them the right of *ius ubique docendi*, in Latin the right to teach throughout the world. Cobban (1975: 26–8) describes the doctorate as a licence to teach anywhere – but a more base reality was closer to home. Teaching had become a monopoly to be enjoyed and exploited by those who conferred the doctorate and by those who attained it (Coulton, 1913: 654).

Doctor of Philosophy

Approximately 100 years after the first doctorates appeared in Europe the doctorate Philosophiae Doctor was recorded at the university in Paris (Green, 1977: 1230). As earlier doctorates had been, it was adopted by other European universities. However, it was not until the nineteenth century in German-speaking parts of Europe (Germany did not come into existence until 1871 after the Franco–Prussian war) that the modern doctor of philosophy degree gained prominence.

Undoubtedly, this new doctorate was further shaped by Humboldt's efforts. In German-speaking institutions the '. . . doctorate gradually replaced the earlier title of Magister, and it became the only recognized degree for the completion of a course of study in the faculty of arts or philosophy' (Lockmiller, 1971: 31). This doctorate was said to consist of two groups of studies – the *quadrivium* (arithmetic, astronomy, geometry, music), and the *trivium* (dialectic/logic, grammar, rhetoric). But according to Coulton (1913: 659) the *quadrivium* group of studies was '. . . never taken very seriously, and by far the most important was the Aristotelian philosophy – hence the ordinary German term of Philosophiae Doctor for Master of Arts.'

Three significant changes in the doctor of philosophy degree have occurred since it appeared at the university in Paris and since it was soundly established at the university in Berlin. One, a written thesis has become a requirement for the degree, whereas originally students presented their theses verbally for public disputation (Schachner, 1962: 322–30). Two, the degree no longer signifies the holder's competence only in philosophy, as it did in earlier years when the liberal arts faculties were labelled philosophy to distinguish them from the professional faculties of law, medicine and theology. Three, whereas the older European doctor of philosophy doctorate was bestowed on those considered to be at their intellectual peak, the contemporary doctorate signifies the holder possesses academically acceptable abilities to commence independent scholarly investigations.

In a speech cited in a study of American and German universities, a graduate who had received a doctor of philosophy degree in Germany is recorded to have said:

> The scholar is expected, first of all, to think for himself and to develop an independent and critical mastery of whatever subject he may have at hand. Next he is expected to *know all that has been learned* up to his day in respect to this subject, and to this purpose to know and digest the literature pertaining to it. Lastly, by personal contact with the original facts, by seeing for himself, and by examining them by the best methods and in the most thorough way, he is expected to *learn something not yet known*, and thus to *add to the sum of human knowledge*. The great principle upon which the method and details of educational process are grounded is that education should fit a man to do this, in fact render it an inner necessity that he should do it.
>
> (Thwing, 1928: 58; emphasis added)

As italicized, the key points of this speech are the three fundamental components of the doctoral degree. Students wanting to become doctors had to conduct original research preceded by and predicated upon a lengthy study of all existing knowledge related to a subject, and they had to prepare and defend a thesis that added to the knowledge of the subject, and which was later published as a book. Lockmiller (1971: 26) describes how candidates had to '. . . prepare a thesis in Latin and defend it in public against a doctor of their college, selected opponents and the general public.'

Conclusion

Doctoral degrees have a long and consistent attainment history. They have propagated in type and number and the doctor of philosophy degree is now the most common. With respect to all doctoral programmes there is an associated 800-year history, which means each programme has considerable educational inertia as part of its existence. Consequently, amendments or changes to the attainment process of the doctoral degree will not be easy to implement in traditional universities. Especially if retention of the historical characteristics of the doctorate is desired.

2

International Spread

PhDs are as much in an international market as currency.
(Professor The Earl Russell)

The doctoral degree spread from Paris to be adopted by universities across Europe, and in German-speaking institutions the research component was emphasized. It is noteworthy that doctoral education in France developed a distinct characteristic with different doctorates being offered at the universities and at the higher order Grandes Ecoles.

Although it had been possible to attain a master degree in Britain, and a doctoral degree by the 1860s, the attainment of the preferred doctor of philosophy degree only became possible in the early part of the twentieth century. As will be revealed, the availability of the doctor of philosophy degree in Britain occurred as a result of educational developments in the United States and Canada, requests from Australia, and defence needs arising from the First World War.

In this chapter, four countries will be considered in the following order: United States, Canada, Britain, then Australia. These countries were selected because their universities have similar academic structures, their doctoral degree programmes have a common ancestry, and the majority of their doctoral programmes are given in the English language.

United States

In the early nineteenth century the United States was still a young nation without graduate-level institutions, and as the Civil War (1861–5) set the country in turmoil for several years, those wishing to study at an advanced level were compelled to leave the country. In most cases, Americans travelled to continental Europe, and this continued even after research qualifications became available in Britain at the end of the nineteenth century. In Britain, a research degree was either a special undergraduate qualification or it required a very long period of time for completion. For example, in 1895 the Doctor Litterarum and the Doctor Philosophiae were described in the records of Aberdeen, Edinburgh, Glasgow and St

Andrews universities, and research baccalaureate degrees were available at Cambridge, London and Oxford (Simpson, 1983: 56, 65, 68, 69, 90).

Because of these reasons Americans generally preferred not to study in Britain. Simpson (69) qualifies this by stating, '. . . a five-year Scottish doctorate compared most unfavourably with the two-year German PhD, or even the one- or two-year research bachelorships of Oxford or Cambridge.'

Clearly, the number of Americans choosing to study in Europe was high. Thwing (1928: 42, 43) writes '(i)t has been estimated that about 10,000 Americans made academic pilgrimages during the nineteenth century and more than half of them studied in the departments of philosophy at German universities . . .'

By the middle of the nineteenth century the doctor of philosophy degree had been introduced to the United States by American graduates returning from Europe. Rosenhaupt and Pinch (1971: 118) record the first doctoral degree in the United States was awarded *honoris causa* at Bucknell University in 1852, whereas the first earned doctorates were conferred by Yale University in 1861 (Xerox University Microfilms, 1973: 864, 991, 1064). For additional details the reader is referred to Appendix A. After the founding of Johns Hopkins University in 1876, the universities in Europe, and particularly those in Germany, were no longer the only possibilities for those students in the United States desirous of attaining the doctor of philosophy degree (Green, 1977: 1235).

Rosenhaupt and Pinch (1971: 118) have described the requirements for the early doctor of philosophy degrees in the United States as, '. . . two years of post-baccalaureate study, a final examination, a thesis, and proficiency in Greek and Latin . . .' By the end of the nineteenth century the components had been strengthened, and two years of resident graduate study plus a thesis '. . . embodying the results of original research bearing the written acceptance of the professor or department in charge' were required (Spurr, 1970: 118, 119).

The doctor of philosophy degree quickly assumed a very high and desirable status, which in turn caused some individuals to question its value. Slosson (1910: 490–6) believed that the doctorate would suffer because of its popularity and that the financial value of the qualification was becoming inflated. James (1903) claimed the doctorate fostered academic snobbery.

By the beginning of the twentieth century, however, the doctor of philosophy degree had become almost a mandatory qualification for professorial appointment at leading universities in the United States (Veysey, 1965: 176); with rare exceptions it is mandatory today. In a document published by the National Academy of Sciences, Harmon (1978: 1) states that the growth in the number of doctor of philosophy degrees conferred has consistently increased at an average of seven per cent per year since the doctorate was first awarded in the United States.

The process of obtaining a doctor of philosophy degree at a contemporary university in the United States is described as follows:

> In general, obtaining a PhD involves 20 or more increasingly specialized courses (may include master degree level courses), conducting research on a very narrow subject, and writing a dissertation that describes the research and its results. The course work usually takes several years to complete even though it is equivalent to three years of academic credit. Classes are usually smaller than undergraduate classes and seminars are common. Typically, students must study articles in scholarly journals as well as textbooks; research papers are usually required. Graduate students have closer contact with their professors and other students in their departments than do undergraduates, but usually have less contact with other parts of university life. They tend to live off campus, are often married, and, in many cases, have jobs or assistantship duties in addition to their studies.
>
> (Braddock, 1987: 2)

Originally promoted by Humboldt as a way of generating knowledge and strengthening a military state, the doctor of philosophy degree in the United States fulfils similar and other needs. The Council of Graduate Schools (1977: 1) states that the degree prepares students for a '. . . lifetime of intellectual inquiry that manifests itself in creative scholarship and research, often leading to careers in social, governmental, business, and industrial organizations as well as the more traditional career in university and college teaching.'

Four significant developments related to doctoral degrees occurred in the United States. Without implying order they are:

First, with respect to the requirement that the thesis be published, the thesis has historically always been published in some form. According to Durant (1957: 341), '(t)he practice of announcing theses, which the proponent offered to defend against all challengers . . .' was an established procedure in medieval universities. It was the same custom that compelled Martin Luther to affix his ninety-five theses to the door of a Wittenberg church in 1517. Rosenhaupt and Pinch (1971: 120) point out that until the 1930s in the United States all theses had to be printed for dissemination, but this was slowly discontinued throughout the 1940s and by the mid-1950s publishing was achieved through the use of microfilm, which is now the normal procedure.

The second development was the widespread granting of doctorates to women. Degrees described as first degrees were conferred on 11 women attending Georgia Female College in 1840, and subsequently, the first female to qualify for a doctoral degree in a research institution received her doctorate from Boston University in 1877 (Lockmiller, 1971: 29, 30). Since then the number of female doctoral graduates has risen from approximately nine per cent of all graduates in the period 1900–4, to 20.5 per cent in 1974 (Harmon, 1978: 17), to 43.8 per cent in 1991 (Ries and Thurgood,

1993: 43). It is projected that by 2001 more females than males will graduate with a doctoral degree in the United States (Hodges, 1991: 11).

It is significant that women were enrolled at the Pythagorean school in the sixth century BC (Durant, 1939: 161); that in Alexandria, Hypatia was a brilliant teacher of mathematics and philosophy up until her death in AD 415 (McLeish, 1992: 91, 92); that women attended Italian universities in the thirteenth century and in the fourteenth century the university at Bologna had female professors (Durant, 1950: 917).

The third development was related to the requirement of competence in two or three languages. This historical requirement has lost support over several decades. Originally, the candidate was expected to know Greek and Latin, which were later replaced by French and German; subsequently, fluency was replaced by a reading knowledge of both, then proficiency in one, and finally to today where research-related courses are an acceptable option (Rosenhaupt and Pinch, 1971: 120). In a study of administrators employed in universities in the United States, Graves (1983: 38) found 53.6 per cent believed that proficiency in a foreign language should be a requirement for all graduate degrees. However, the majority dismissed a return to French or German, and approved other languages, Russian for example.

Professionalization is the fourth development. In German-speaking universities the practice of equating the doctor of philosophy degree with research was well established (on this point, LaPidus (1990: 21) describes the important difference between the generation of knowledge and information) and the degree was viewed differently from the professional doctorates associated with law, medicine and theology. However, in the United States unique conditions produced a change in focus. Walters (1965: 4) describes how early '(f)rontier conditions had moulded the American people into a primarily practical-minded people, and instruction in industrial, mechanical and agricultural arts began to be demanded.'

Hand-in-hand with this was the need of the developing professions to have an adequate and constant number of qualified graduates to execute the responsibilities of these professions, and to foster research that would improve their practice (Mayhew, 1977: 1907). The new reality and demands of a developing nation strained the old and traditional concept of the doctoral degree. Dewey (1917: 31) saw a conflict between a '. . . technical and specialized training . . .' and the educational endeavour '. . . to live in the past by way of inviting the soul of our youth to a leisurely and liberal culture.'

Although Humboldt promoted the doctor of philosophy degree to prepare scholars and scientists, which is in reality training for a profession (Bent, 1959), the degree has become available in an array of professional subjects, for example '. . . accounting, animal science, home economics, education, German, nursing, nuclear engineering, physical education, veterinary pathology and zoology' (Walters, 1965: viii). There are now over 50 distinct doctoral degrees offered in the United States (see Table 2.1).

Table 2.1   Research doctoral degrees offered in US (1991)

DA	Doctor of Arts	DMin/DM	Doctor of Ministry
DAS	Doctor of Applied Science	DML	Doctor of Modern Languages
DArch	Doctor of Architecture	DM	Doctor of Music
DBA	Doctor of Business Administration	DMA	Doctor of Music Arts
JCD	Doctor of Canon Law	DME	Doctor of Music Education
DChem	Doctor of Chemistry	DMM	Doctor of Music Ministry
DCL	Doctor of Comparative Law/Civil Law	DNSc	Doctor of Nursing Science
DCJ	Doctor of Criminal Justice	PhD	Doctor of Philosophy
DCrim	Doctor of Criminology	DPE	Doctor of Physical Education
DrDes	Doctor of Design	DPS	Doctor of Professional Studies
EdD	Doctor of Education	DPA	Doctor of Public Administration
DEnv	Doctor of Environment	DPH	Doctor of Public Health
DED	Doctor of Environmental Design	DRec/DR	Doctor of Recreation
DEng	Doctor of Engineering	RhD	Doctor of Rehabilitation
DESc/ScDE	Doctor of Engineering Science	DRE	Doctor of Religious Education
DFA	Doctor of Fine Arts	DSM	Doctor of Sacred Music
DF	Doctor of Forestry	STD	Doctor of Sacred Theology
DGS	Doctor of Geological Science	DSc/ScD	Doctor of Science
DHS	Doctor of Health and Safety	DScH	Doctor of Science and Hygiene
DHL	Doctor of Hebrew Letters/ Literature	DScD	Doctor of Science in Dentistry
DHS	Doctor of Hebrew Studies	DScVM	Doctor of Science in Veterinary Medicine
DIT	Doctor of Industrial Technology	LScD	Doctor of Science of Law
SJD	Doctor of Juridical Science	DSSc	Doctor of Social Science
JSD	Doctor of Juristic Science	DSW	Doctor of Social Work
DLS	Doctor of Library Science	ThD	Doctor of Theology
DMSc	Doctor of Medical Science		

Source: Ries and Thurgood (1993: 131)

Two points encompass the development of the doctor of philosophy degree in the United States: **1** Refinement – standardization of quality, elimination of the honorary degree appellation, prolongation and intensification of the study period; **2** Expansion – equal acceptance of females and the option of a broad range of academic subjects.

For Scott (1984: 3), the doctoral degree was introduced '. . . to wean wealthy Americans off the universities of Germany.' The fact that 359 institutions in the United States now offer doctorates attests to its success (Ries and Thurgood, 1993: 84–9).

Canada

To the north in Canada the foundations for a doctoral degree were laid over several decades. Like their American cousins, Canadians had been attracted by the possibilities that existed at universities across the Atlantic. Ross (1975: 197) claims that '(d)uring the 1870s Canadians who were concerned about improving higher education looked to Europe for inspiration.'

By the end of the nineteenth century, however, Britain had lost its appeal owing to its inability to provide the short research oriented doctorate. It was stated by Young (1903: 7) that '. . . Oxford has ceased to be the intellectual centre of the Empire . . .' whereas the German university system retained its revered position. In an 1880 article cited by Ross (1975: 197) a correspondent wrote, '. . . both in the quantity and quality of her original scientific work, Germany has far outstripped any other nation,' to emphasize the quality of the universities in Germany.

Canadians who had completed a doctorate out of the country returned home and started improving undergraduate education in their own institutions. Towards the end of the nineteenth century interest in continental European universities also began to wane, although not completely, as increased attention was being given to developments taking place to the south in the United States (Adams, 1887; Gordy, 1891). And according to Mayhew (1977: 1913), 'Canadian professors encouraged their more able students to migrate to the United States for graduate work'.

Over time a small number of Canadian graduates returned home and began to suggest doctoral programmes be established in Canada. At least one returning student extolled the benefits of doctoral education in the United States and urged the University of Toronto to introduce a similar programme (Hunter, 1880).

Slowly, educational nationalism became a rallying cry. In his history of higher education in Canada, Harris (1976: 187) writes that '(t)he 1890–91 calendars of three Canadian universities, Mount Allison, New Brunswick and Queen's, outline a program for the PhD.' He points out that the same Mount Allison calendar records two doctoral degrees being granted, but it appears that both recipients, staff professors, received the degrees as honorary titles.

Drawing on these developments and following the lead of the establishment of Johns Hopkins University in 1876, and the University of

Chicago in 1891, both of which had research as their *raison d'être*, educational reformers at the University of Toronto began to push for the adoption of a doctoral degree. In 1894 James Louden, then president, succeeded in having the DPaed (Doctor Paedagogiae) offered at Toronto, and after much lobbying the university senate finally approved the doctor of philosophy degree in 1897 (Ross, 1975: 194). Louden's efforts were hampered by the small number of doctoral graduates that could be employed in Canadian institutions, as higher education was not growing at a rate similar to that in the United States (Squair, 1904).

As an indication of the demand for academic staff, Ross (1976: 26) records that in 1850 Canada had ten institutions called universities and the United States had 800. Although it seems reasonable to believe the latter figure probably included degree-granting colleges, institutions granting undergraduate qualifications only, the demand for staff in Canada was indisputably smaller than in the United States.

At McGill University the doctor of philosophy degree appeared nine years after it was offered at the University of Toronto (Frost, 1967), although the availability of two earned doctorates, the Doctor Litterarum and the Doctor Scientiarum, preceded it (Harris, 1976: 312).

By 1906 the requirements for the doctor of philosophy in Canadian universities had been standardized. The requirements were three years of full-time study beyond the baccalaureate degree; a major and two minor subjects; one outside major subject; a reading knowledge of French and German; a comprehensive examination in the major field; plus a thesis. Doctoral theses embodied 'the results of original investigation' at the University of Toronto, and represented a 'distinct contribution to knowledge' at McGill (Harris, 1976: 431). Canadian doctor of philosophy diplomas were first conferred at the University of Toronto on three male students in 1900 and two female students in 1903 (Mills and Dombra, 1968: 24, 131). For additional details the reader is referred to Appendix A. Although the availability of this doctorate in Canada did not stop all prospective doctoral students from leaving the country, it greatly reduced the number.

The early influence of the German doctorate in the formulation of the academic requirements for the Canadian doctor of philosophy degree is readily evident in a speech delivered to the Royal Society of Canada:

As to the ultimate scientific value of what has already been accomplished in the way of research under the influence of this recent movement (the rapid development of graduate programmes in the USA), there is room for a qualifying remark. It must be remembered that much of the graduate work referred to does not mean actual research, the course for the PhD in many cases being no higher than the honours BA course with us. What is required to remedy this unsatisfactory condition is that the PhD be given only on the German plan, and that the main test therefore, a research, be published. When this condition becomes absolute there will be material for the world's judgement as to the amount and quality of the contribution to the advancement of knowledge.

(Louden, 1902: vi)

In Canada there was little demand for doctoral degree holders during the First World War, the Great Depression, and the Second World War. From 1950 to 1975, however, there was unprecedented growth in the size of Canadian universities (McNeal, Hodysh and Konrad, 1981: C21) as students from the post-war population boom arrived on campuses across the nation. This growth spurred on the development of doctoral degree programmes. In 1944–5 only five universities offered these programmes, but by 1978 the number had risen to 34 (Zur-Muehlen, 1978: 71).

This growth prompted Bonneau and Corry (1972: 54) to state that '(t)oo many departments in too many universities are offering PhD programs they are not equipped to mount, to the detriment of graduate work in the country as a whole.' Since the 1970s the number has dropped and 31 universities across Canada now offer the doctoral degree (Archer, 1992: 1020–550).

Fifteen years ago, Zur-Muehlen (1978: 83) calculated that in Canada only 'one out of four of the 2000 new PhDs produced each year will be absorbed as replacements for PhD holders who retire, die or withdraw for health reasons.' Accentuating this is the fact that compulsory retirement based on age has been successfully challenged in the courts, which will inevitably slow the rate of absorption.

This situation is less favourable than that which now exists in the United States. The overall employment picture there is promising for most, but definitely not all, doctoral graduates. Bestor (1982: 251) has assessed that in the United States '(b)etween 1980 and 2000, only one in ten holders of humanities doctorates will ever find academic employment, with not all of these finding jobs leading to tenure and a permanent career.'

Britain

If educational nationalism stimulated the adoption of the doctoral degree by universities in Canada, then political nationalism stimulated its acceptance by British universities.

Certainly all of the older universities in Britain were moulded, logically, on the two university archetypes that existed in continental Europe. The University of Oxford, established *circa* 1167, was in its early years influenced by the university in Paris according to McNeal, Hodysh and Konrad (1981: C15) who cite Rashdall's (1936) scholarly work on medieval universities. Whereas at the university in Glasgow, founded in 1451, the intent was to use the university at Bologna as the model to follow (Coulton, 1913: 654). Historically, the emphasis in British universities was placed on teaching, not on research. Emphasis on conducting research, which first gained prominence in German-speaking universities and which was later adopted by universities in the United States, then Canada, was generally not of primary and widespread importance at the universities in Britain until the early to mid-twentieth century; emphasis being given to high quality baccalaurate education.

However, a number of developments paved the way for the provision of the doctor of philosophy degree. Rudd and Simpson (1975: 9) identify the University of Durham where a MSc (Magister Scientiarum) degree was introduced in 1878, and where four years later a more senior degree, the DSc (Doctor Scientiarum) was offered. Other universities in Britain also offered post-baccalaureate programmes:

> By the turn of the century, the British universities were coming to the end of the first stage in the evolution of higher degrees. An earned mastership was available – or about to become available – in most universities other than Oxford and Cambridge; this provided a goal for students wanting to take their studies beyond first-degree level by a year or two. Doctorates were now awarded in most fields; however, these required the student to do some high level research and produce original work of considerable calibre, and, moreover, the thesis could not normally be submitted until at least five years had elapsed after the first degree. Unlike Germany and North America, Britain did not yet have the lower doctorate that could be gained after two or three years' research, the PhD. This degree was originally introduced in Germany, well before the nineteenth century, and had taken a form which is somewhat different from that to which we are now accustomed in Britain.
>
> (Rudd and Simpson, 1975: 9, 10)

With respect to this British reference to a lower doctorate and by implication the existence of a higher doctorate, some institutions in the United States and Canada have granted the DSc degree as an honorary award. Spurr (1970: 16, 17) claims '(t)his practice is particularly unfortunate since the DSc in England, other British Commonwealth countries, the USSR and elsewhere is the highest earned doctorate, substantially above the PhD in measurement of maturity and scientific accomplishment.' Later works referring to doctoral degrees in Britain (Kogan Page, 1985: 49, 50) as well as the USSR (Holmes, 1987: 10) support Spurr's claim.

But ultimately what brought the doctor of philosophy degree to Britain was political nationalism. Assisting the process were several significant related events. In 1916 the chairman of a conference of Canadian universities is quoted by Sartain (1955: 482) as saying that only through the 'establishment of doctorates that may be obtained within a reasonable time, and by subvention through scholarships, can we hope that the stream of students which of late has set towards the United States will be diverted to the universities of Britain.'

For although Canadian academics still encouraged their brighter students to undertake post-baccalaureate study in the United States, others involved with higher education were not in favour of Canadian students going south of the border. Too many graduates did not return. University officials felt that if Canadian students could study in Britain there would be an increased likelihood they would return home at the completion of their studies. Whereas for those students who studied in the United States, and who subsequently stayed there, going home to Canada only necessitated a short and convenient train trip.

To achieve this diversion Canadian university administrators participated in several conferences in Britain leading up to the First Congress of Universities of the Empire, which was held in Britain in 1912 (Rudd and Simpson, 1975: 12). At this congress a direct proposal that British universities offer the doctor of philosophy degree was made. This pressure exerted by colonial universities, in conjunction with the fact that British students were also going to Europe to study, softened academic resistance.

A strong objection to the degree was expressed by the University of London because '. . . the conditions of study proposed for it were very similar to those of the London master's degree' (Rudd and Simpson, 1975: 13). From 1860 onwards a DSc degree had also been available at that university (Simpson, 1983: 37). But the doctor of philosophy degree was inevitably introduced to Britain, its introduction hastened by the First World War.

This confrontation prevented students from travelling to Germany. It also showed how sophisticated and effective German science had become. To those in Britain holding positions of influence and political importance it was unthinkable that Germany could have risen to such high academic stature, which in turn had aided it to exert military power and economic domination over much of Europe. On this point Lord Blackett (1969: 1) said, '(t)he dominance of Germany in the pure sciences including medicine during the last half of the nineteenth and the beginning of the twentieth centuries must have owed much to the institution of the Doctorate as an award for research achievement.'

So, with mixed opinions, the doctor of philosophy degree was adopted. In her account of the event Simpson (1983: 135) writes, 'Oxford was indeed the first British university to award the PhD or – as in its traditionally individualistic fashion it designates it – the DPhil.' Buckingham, Sussex, (Ulster) and York universities also use the DPhil designation.

At the University of Cambridge a somewhat similar process prevailed. Strong academic demands coming from outside the institution and a wartime environment, pressured the institution to offer the doctor of philosophy degree. A report presented at a Syndicate meeting convened to discuss the issue in 1918 reads as follows:

It said little on the general problem that was new or that has not already been mentioned in this note, but it repeated with emphasis, evidence and authority, the following propositions: (i) There has been a widespread practice in the universities of Canada and the United States, by which graduates have pursued their studies partly in their own and partly in other universities. (ii) Before the war the majority of those who left their own country for such a purpose went to German universities. (iii) There is a general desire in the United States and the Dominions that in future the flow of such students should be directed to a much greater extent than at present to British universities. (iv) It is essential that such students should not only find suitable conditions for pursuing their studies, but should also be able to obtain definite recognition of their work. (v) It is indispensable that such recognition should take the form of a Doctor's degree. The Syndicate added that they had come to the conclusion that the title of the degree should be Philosophiae Doctor (PhD) for the reasons that this title was the one in general use for the purpose in North America and elsewhere, and that it would mark the degree as quite distinct from the doctorates given at the time by this University; the title would cover both literary and scientific studies.

(Sartain, 1955)

The final outcome was that Cambridge adopted this degree in 1919 and conferred it for the first time in 1921 (Waller, 1992), one year after Oxford had conferred the first doctor of philosophy degree in Britain (Bailey, 1989). For additional details the reader is referred to Appendix A. In British universities this doctorate is considered an earned research degree. Academic course work, as undertaken in North America, is not normally required, and the preparation of the thesis necessitates lengthy study and research of a high calibre. At Oxford, for example, the thesis must make a 'significant and substantial contribution' in the field selected by the candidate (Kogan Page, 1985: 49, 50).

This emphasis on the thesis has been criticized for being too rigid and irrelevant to future careers. A Dr Warren, reported to be from the Rockefeller Foundation, is quoted by Surridge (1989: 2) as saying the entire British system 'should be loosened up and the thesis dropped.' In the 1980s the issue of mandatory taught courses again became a national higher education concern (Ash *et al.*, 1988: 2); the matter being raised 20 years earlier in the Swann (1968) report submitted to the British parliament by the Secretary of State for Education and Science, and the Minister of Technology. Today, 96 universities, which includes 40 former polytechnics, can confer the doctoral degree in Britain (Archer, 1992: 382–1015; Clarke, 1993).

Australia

Of the four countries, Australia was the last to offer a doctoral degree. Like students from the United States and Canada, Australian residents were compelled to travel overseas to study for a doctorate. To facilitate this, Australian officials took part in two significant gatherings held in Britain – the Allied Colonial Universities Conference, 1903, and the Imperial Conference on Education, 1907 (Rudd and Simpson, 1975: 11).

At these meetings the issue of colonial undergraduate degrees as acceptable entry degrees for graduate study was discussed. By 1918 most British universities had accepted Australian qualifications as graduate entry requirements (Rudd and Simpson, 1975: 13). Hill and Johnston (1984: 122) claim doctoral education was slow in developing because of the 'traditional cultural cringe to overseas universities for higher level education.' A good example is the physical sciences, where until 1970 one examiner for the doctorate had to be from out of the country (Hill, Fensham and Howden, 1974: 14).

But this perspective developed not solely from a colonial obsequiousness, but from a combination of academic inadequacies in the yet-young universities (for example, library facilities), and the belief that the doctoral degree signified and necessitated a broad international education. A programme undertaken at an isolated university in an isolated country was deemed not in keeping with the meaning of the degree. The argument for studying abroad, particularly in the humanities, is eloquently stated thus:

> There is the conviction that in most of the Arts subjects a PhD ought to be done abroad, that no one should have a doctorate in German who has not studied in Germany, that no one should have a doctorate in English who has not studied in the great libraries of England and experienced life and tradition at first hand. Apart from such reasons, which might be adduced for every subject, there is the general principle that a PhD in Arts should be proof of first-hand knowledge of the European home of our civilizations and traditions and of a scholar's exposure to other influences than those operating in his own university. At the PhD level, it is believed, scholarship should operate and should be experienced at the international, cosmopolitan level. In many subjects, of which modern, foreign and classical languages are obvious examples, a PhD done entirely in Australia would, even if satisfying the accepted PhD requirements, have a regrettable parochial limitation about it.

> (Mitchell, 1959: 86)

Exacerbated by staff shortages, this situation persisted until after the Second World War. Slowly, a national attitude towards doctoral education evolved. An Australian encyclopedia (Grolier Society, 1983: 134) shows that the acceptance of the doctor of philosophy degree was delayed until 1945, and archival records confirm this doctorate was first awarded at the universities of Melbourne in 1948 (Arthur, 1989) and Sydney in 1951 (Smith, 1989). For additional details the reader is referred to Appendix A. Note that in nearby New Zealand it appears the first doctor of philosophy degree was conferred in 1927 (Stone, 1990).

This delay resulted in the establishment of very sound master degrees. Today, doctoral programmes in Australia are similar to British and North American programmes. Students normally commence their programme after completing a master degree or honours baccalaureate degree, emphasis is placed on the thesis, and taught courses are not generally required.

After deliberating on doctoral education in Australia in the 1990s, one observer in Australia writes:

> The lack of any significant formal course work within our PhD, and master degrees by research has continued for three decades. The focus of our PhD research type degrees continues to be the research project, and this is almost the only medium by which education is accomplished.
>
> (Stranks, 1984: 171)

Stranks discusses the inclusion of taught courses within a doctoral programme, and claims these courses need not be as extensive as in the United States because of the stringent demands of the Australian master degree. Doctoral degrees are now offered in 29 Australian institutions (Archer, 1992: 1–324).

Conclusion

Doctoral degrees have been adopted in Australia, Britain, Canada and the United States. Due to historical, geographical and economic reasons many different types of doctorates now exist in the United States. Although specific regulations and requirements vary, for additional details the reader is referred to Appendix B, all reputable universities in these countries require the completion of three fundamental components for the awarding of a traditional doctoral degree. These components are lengthy study, original research and thesis preparation.

3
Contemporary Problems

A problem is something you have hopes of changing.

(C. R. Smith)

Doctoral degrees are being questioned. On the university campus, in the business community and within the political realm doctoral degrees have been and continue to be discussed; often negatively. Internationally, doctoral programmes are being challenged and criticized.

As evidence of contemporary problems, brief details related to ten contentious issues related to doctoral degrees are examined here. These problems include appropriateness, attrition, discrimination, employment, entrepreneurship, programme emphasis, research competency evaluation, time to complete, unconventional programmes and writing for publication. They were chosen because related contentions appear periodically in the higher education literature and press.

Whether all the criticism levelled at doctoral programmes and those who hold a doctoral degree is valid is overridden here by its persistent existence. The criticisms are highlighted succinctly and without discussion simply as evidence of the international disharmony and discontent surrounding doctoral degrees. It is beyond the purpose of this book to address in detail all doctoral problems in Australia, Britain, Canada and the United States.

Doctoral Problems

Appropriateness

Strong opposition to the doctor of philosophy degree has been expressed by those who do not consider it an appropriate degree. This opposition has occurred over many years and in a number of countries.

Early this century, James (1903) addressed the proliferation of the doctorate in the United States. He claimed it would require a narrow specialization, whereas a broad cultural and ethical education would be more suitable for undergraduate professors. Sixty years later the echo of this claim was heard in Britain when Lord Robbins *et al.* (1963: 101) concluded the 'insistence on a higher degree or substantial publication' for a junior lectureship would be disastrous.

In the United States today, Smith (1990: 108–22) reveals numerous negative aspects of the degree's appropriateness. During the 1960s and 1970s in Canada, the belief that the doctor of philosophy was the appropriate degree for university professors resulted in a breakdown of planning and coordination among and between universities and governments according to Symons and Page (1984: 29). In Australia, respondents in Sekhon's (1989) study were sceptical about the appropriateness of the same doctorate. Cude (1987: 98) believes the doctorate is overrated, and claims universities have a 'fixation on the PhD as the one true certificate for all scholarly functions.'

Attrition

Attrition of doctoral students/candidates is a long-standing concern. Berelson (1960: 167) quotes Sir Hugh Taylor, the then graduate dean of Princeton University, as saying '(i)f the graduate schools of the country would solve this problem of attrition . . . we could raise substantially the output of the graduate schools of the country without increasing enrollment or additional expenditures for faculty and facilities.'

Rosenhaupt and Pinch (1971: 121) state that 50 per cent of doctoral students do not graduate, a figure reiterated by the Association of American Universities (1990: 2). Garcia (1987: 1) cites eight references and claims 23 to 45 per cent of all graduate students fail in the United States, and Ziolkowski (1990) claims the figure is 70 per cent for doctoral students. In Canada, Smith *et al.* (1991: 103) write that the average doctoral student attrition rate appears to be a third, and that '43 per cent of those starting a doctoral program in Ontario failed to complete the degree within ten years.' In Britain, the Society for Research into Higher Education published a text by Rudd (1985) that addresses attrition, and in the United States, the Council of Graduate Schools (1990a) has published a booklet to prevent the problem.

Discrimination

It is claimed that the female experience of obtaining a doctoral degree is dissimilar to that experienced by males. This results from parental pressures, early school influences and cultural expectations in the opinion of Centra and Kuykendall (1974: 1). Discrimination within the university, based on gender (Levy, 1982) and compounded by racial origin (McLean, 1981), is alleged to occur. Writing on women's experiences, Moore (1985: 84) claims females in graduate school attend programmes that are less prestigious and take longer to finish than those taken by male graduate students, and although 'they may receive an equal amount of financial aid, they are still less likely to receive preferred jobs such as research assistantships which support independent study.'

In a work edited by Vartuli (1982), the common theme is that universities must reconsider their approach to female students. Other authors, both female (Paludi, 1990; Thompson and Roberts, 1985) and male (Anderson, 1992; Sternberg, 1981), looking at this situation see discrimination affecting female university students. To help females, Phillips and Pugh (1987: 131–40) devote a whole chapter to the problem, 'How to Survive in a Predominantly British, White, Male, Full-Time Academic Environment', in their book on the doctor of philosophy degree.

Although the level of discrimination will differ from university to university, discrimination based on gender may be expected to occur in the four countries mentioned. Due to the seriousness of this problem, a list of works related to discrimination has been compiled for the reader in Appendix C.

Employment

For the aspirant to a doctoral degree the opportunity for employment after graduating is an issue. In Canada, Gerson (1989) speaks of a shortage of doctor of philosophy degree holders, but Zur-Muehlen (1987) believes a faculty supply crisis in the 1990s seems unlikely. In Australia, Maslen (1991a) reports an academic staff shortage is imminent. In the United States it is claimed a shortage will occur in the 1990s (Bowen and Sosa, 1989; D'Arms, 1990; Mooney, 1989a) and that there will be a demand for over 500,000 new academics during the period from 1985 to 2010 (Bowen and Schuster, 1986: 188–200).

It is of interest that in the 1970s the concern in Australia (Davies, 1972), Canada (Repo, 1970) and the United States (Chambers, 1976; Wolfe and Kidd, 1971) was the glut of doctoral graduates – the alarming oversupply of graduates and their subsequent under-employment (Kerr, 1975; Wilcox, 1975).

In Britain, research funding cutbacks have created difficulties for aspiring academics. Fisher (1987: 13) states 'if the current crisis does not result in the right environment then perhaps the most sensitive indicator of job strain will be brain drain.' At a recent meeting of the Association of Learned Societies in the Social Sciences in Britain, a claim was made that '(n)othing in current research training encourages employers to value recruits with PhDs' (Gold, 1988: 7). This can only compound the employment problem.

Thompson and Roberts (1985: 2) write, '(t)oday the academic picture is catastrophic for all unemployed and untenured academicians, female and male.' It appears that not all doctoral degree holders will find appropriate employment in the future.

Entrepreneurship

Yet another issue that causes debate is what constitutes an appropriate activity for those holding or seeking a doctoral degree. For would-be holders of a doctorate and the institutions that employ them, the lure of financial rewards may induce some to establish enterprises and to obtain patents on processes and products that can then be exploited to make money, according to Norris (1989).

Problems inherent in entrepreneurship have been described in the Canadian literature. Helwig (1988: 48) quotes an assistant professor as saying, 'any new academic is putting in 50- to 60-hour weeks . . . if you try to be entrepreneurial on top of that, something has to give.' Entrepreneurship was predicted by Clark Kerr when he was president of the University of California in the 1960s. He saw knowledge as the growth area in the American economy and the professor taking on entrepreneurial characteristics (Draper, 1965: 63). In Britain, commercial developments involving universities are now causing concern (*Times Higher Education Supplement*, 1991: 32).

Programme emphasis

In a study of higher education institutions in the United States, Berelson (1960: 290) found one third of the responding graduate deans believed that research was over emphasized in graduate programmes; Smith (1990: 178, 189) also says that research and the publishing of research findings are over emphasized in universities. Reporting on the rationalization of research in Canada, Bonneau and Corry (1972: 58) describe a difference in opinions on what is the appropriate research emphasis for the doctor of philosophy degree, 'essentially a training in methods', or an 'apprenticeship on the upper slopes of the unclimbed peaks of knowledge'.

Writing on the educational reform of American education, Vandament (1988: A52) states that doctoral programmes should 'include coverage of educational policy issues, the teaching–learning process, and the history of higher education'. In the United States, Stine (1989) describes the need for doctoral students to undertake practice teaching as part of their programmes. Educational reformers in Britain are calling for changes to the doctorate and are advocating taught courses as part of doctoral degree programmes, similar to North American programmes (Williams, 1988). An Australian Academy of Science document describes how some programmes emphasize socialization into a profession, and how this process is an important part of doctoral education (Hill, Fensham and Howden, 1974: 34–41).

Research competency evaluation

Russell G. Hamilton, as graduate school dean of Vanderbilt University, is quoted as saying that the thesis is 'the major stumbling block to the PhD' (Monaghan, 1989: A1). After investigating this problem, the Council of Graduate Schools (1991) released a booklet titled, *The Role and Nature of the Doctoral Dissertation*.

Halstead (1987) recommends the research competence of doctoral students be assessed through a series of smaller projects, rather than on the solitary big project or thesis. This is contested by those who believe the whole point of a doctoral programme is the thesis; the information services director of the American Anthropological Association is reported by Monaghan (1986: A16) to have said 'one big dissertation is a rite of passage, and is the one big test.'

Alternate methods of evaluating research competence are now accepted at some institutions. At several universities in the United States papers published in refereed journals or as works in edited volumes are approved options to the thesis. Other examples of options are the imaginative writing thesis that is acceptable at the University of Iowa, or a published work at the University of Cambridge. In Britain, some universities have recommended the thesis be replaced with courses (Williams, 1988), and in the United States, Solomon and Solomon (1993: 108, 109) have recently suggested the thesis be dropped as a doctoral degree component.

Time to complete

Concern is expressed over the time it takes students to complete the doctoral degree. Full-time students attending British universities are now expected to finish in four years or less (Winfield, 1987). Cambridge has been on a 'blacklist of institutions where ESRC (Economic and Social Research Council) studentships can no longer be held because fewer than 40 per cent of Cambridge's doctor of philosophy students have managed to complete their degree in the prescribed four-year period' (Heron, 1989: 1). Cambridge was subsequently removed from this list as a result of improved completion rates (Richards, 1991: 5). A recent report on completion times indicates that doctoral students in Australia lag behind their counterparts enrolled in British universities (Maslen 1991b: 10).

A similar criticism comes from the Canadian Manufacturers' Association (1986), whose science and technology committee claims the time to complete a doctorate is too long. In an effort to prevent this, the Canadian Association of Graduate Schools has prepared a policy requesting that

Table 3.1   Years to complete doctoral degree in US*

	1957^1	1967^2	1977^2	1987^2	1991^3	%#
Education	5.2	6.2	6.4	7.9	8.1	56
Engineering	4.3	5.2	5.6	5.8	6.1	42
Humanities	6.0	5.5	7.1	8.4	8.4	40
Life sciences	4.2	5.4	5.7	6.5	6.7	60
Physical sciences	4.5	5.1	5.7	6.0	6.3	40
Professional/other	5.0	5.3	6.1	7.2	7.5	50
Mean for all fields	5.0	5.4	6.1	6.9	7.0	40

* Registered time to degree – graduate registration to graduation
\# Percentage increase in time from 1957 to 1991

Sources: [1] Berelson (1960: 158)
[2] Coyle and Thurgood (1989: 31)
[3] Ries and Thurgood (1993: 16)

universities assist students in expediting their doctoral programmes (Maclachlan, 1987). In a recent national document the principal researcher reports it takes an 'astonishingly long period of time' to obtain a doctor of philosophy degree in Canada (Smith *et al.*, 1991: 101).

Evangelauf (1989: A1) claims administrators are troubled by the increasing amount of time students are taking to complete their doctoral degree, which 'can deter undergraduates from considering doctoral study, can demoralize those already enrolled in graduate school and represents an inefficient use of campus resources.' Data is available (see Table 3.1) that shows the time to obtain a doctorate in the United States is increasing; the most recent figures show a minimum of 6.1 years, to a maximum of 8.4 years, with a mean for all fields of 7.0 years.

Kowalski (1987: 10) states, 'too much emphasis is placed on the product rather than the process'. A positive relationship between the student/candidate and adviser/director/supervisor seems crucial for a doctorate to be completed in good time (Buckley and Hooley, 1988; Christopherson *et al.*, 1983; Powles, 1988; Salmon, 1992: 19–28; Wright, 1991).

In the United States, the Alfred P. Sloan Foundation and the Andrew W. Mellon Foundation gave grants in 1991 for studies of completion probabilities and completion times related to doctoral degrees.

Unconventional programmes

Programmes offered in unconventional formats are changing the way some students achieve their doctorate. One that is receiving support is the inter-university doctoral programme. Where once students studied at only one university, some new doctoral programmes accommodate and encourage students to study at several.

In Canada, Concordia University, McGill University, Université de Montréal and the Université du Québec are collaborating on a joint doctoral programme in administration, and Concordia offers a doctoral programme in conjunction with the Nanjing Institute of Technology in the People's Republic of China (Weston, 1988a). This international cooperation, termed jointly-supervised degrees by the British Council (1986: 12, 13) is well established in that country.

In Europe, COMETT – Community in Education and Training for Technology, and ERASMUS – European Action Scheme for the Mobility of University Students, are two unconventional programmes that ensure students can study at several institutions, thereby enriching their educational experience (Massué and Schinck, 1987; Scott, 1989).

A development that is gaining support in the United States is one that does not require students to study on an institutional campus. Apps (1988: 122–45) describes this development, which includes the Electronic University Network based in California, and the National Technological University in Colorado.

Whereas full-time study for at least part of the programme has generally been the historical norm for doctoral degrees, some institutions now facilitate the attainment of doctoral degrees through part-time study, for example, Birkbeck College in Britain and Walden University in the United States.

Writing for publication

Looking at this academic standard of publishing has prompted Bercuson, Bothwell and Granatstein (1984: 108–29) to declare that Canadian academics are not publishing enough. Writing for publication provides valuable experience and exposure for prospective doctoral degree holders wishing to work in a university.

According to Boyer (1988), scholarship is equated with publishing not with teaching, regardless of teaching abilities or the needs of undergraduate students. Chapman and Webster (1993) are critical of this emphasis on publishing.

Evidence that publishing is not a desirable activity amongst all academics exists in the results of two national surveys. Whitney (1987) asked the readers of the Science Council of Canada's newsletter to compare the importance of publishing with the importance of contract research. Over 1,400 readers, approximately 40 per cent of the readership, responded that contract research was either equally or more important than publishing. In the United States, a survey of academics conducted by the Carnegie Foundation for the Advancement of Teaching (Mooney, 1989b) revealed that 28 per cent of faculty had not published a journal article, 57 per cent had never published a book, and that 60 per cent believed that teaching effectiveness should be the primary evaluation criterion for promotion.

Doctor of philosophy problems

Recently the author conducted a prognostic study, hereafter termed the PhD study, related to a doctoral degree (Noble, 1992). As doctoral degrees are international qualifications, a broad panel was identified to take part in the study. All of the scholars who participated have a national or international frame of reference, in addition to personal knowledge of the components, characteristics and conventions of doctoral degrees.

A total of 67 scholars, 15 females and 52 males, from Australia (AU), Britain (BR), Canada (CA), and the United States (US) made up the panel. Readers wanting additional information on the qualifications and positions of the participants involved in the PhD study are referred to Appendix D.

To ensure a range of perspectives, the scholars represented a cross-section of those involved with higher education. This decision was taken to avoid encapsulation bias, which occurs within every discipline and profession, and which restricts the perspective of those practising them (Royce, 1964). Evidence of this bias in universities, and the restrictive outcomes caused by it, has been documented by Becher (1981) and Donald (1983).

In the initial phase of the study the scholars identified the problematic issues associated with the doctor of philosophy degree. Verbatim quotes, short and long, from their responses appear throughout the remainder of the book. Overall, 232 issues were identified and the reader will find them listed in Appendix E. Of these problems, 211 became the focus of attention (see Table 3.2); the remaining 21, which were identified only once, were not included in the study. In the final phase, a two-round questionnaire process, the scholars assessed reiteratively the outcome of 18 solutions proposed to resolve the major problems they identified.

By far the most frequent issue identified was the problem of what constitutes appropriate doctoral research. Comments such as, 'goal of PhD study not agreed upon' (AU), 'new facts over an interpretation' (BR), 'interest and relevance' (CA), and 'too much stress on originality' (US), were some of the 38 problematic issues recorded in this research-related grouping.

A lack of a clearly stated purpose for the required/proposed studies was a problematic issue identified 27 times. Statements such as 'how much study is required?' (AU), 'prescribed courses do not meet the research training needs of the student' (BR), 'courses do not seem to be of any use to the proposed research' (CA), and 'excessive course requirements' (US), were recorded.

Faculty advising/directing/supervising formed the third largest group, and this issue was identified 26 times. Comments such as, 'supervisors and students fail to define sensible and manageable projects which can be completed' (AU), 'poor staff understanding' (BR), 'supervision is too permissive' (CA), and 'professors prolong the process because of overwhelming concern about total perfection' (US), were comments in this group.

Table 3.2   PhD problems identified in international PhD study

Problematic issue	Frequency	Country			
		AU	BR	CA	US
What is appropriate doctoral research	38	X	X	X	X
Purpose of study/courses	27	X	X	X	X
Faculty advising/directing/supervising	26	X	X	X	X
Breadth/content/depth/scope of thesis not adequately defined	18	X	X	X	X
Quality of writing in theses	16	X	X	X	X
Financial support	12			X	X
Study of research methods	11	X	X	X	X
Alternatives to thesis	10	X		X	X
Time to complete thesis	8	X	X	X	X
Part-time students	8	X		X	X
Length of thesis	8	X		X	X
Insufficient suitable courses	5	X		X	X
Interdisciplinary emphasis	5			X	X
Time to complete entire degree	4	X	X	X	X
Creativity in thought restricted	4	X			X
Research not 'collaborative'	4				X
Practical component	3			X	X
Foreign languages needed	2				X
Failure to provide teacher training	2				X
	211				

Source: Noble (1992: 85)

The issue of the thesis was identified as a problem 18 times. Specifically, the breadth, the content, the depth, and the scope of the thesis are not thought to be defined adequately. Problems such as 'the standards by which theses are to be judged are incredibly vague' (AU), 'reducing the scope of a thesis to a manageable size' (BR), 'a committee of professors who may have different notions of what constitutes a thesis' (CA), and 'preparation for a career versus a magnum opus' (US) were listed.

The poor quality of writing, grammar, punctuation, syntax, etc., in theses was identified 16 times. Statements included, 'theses are not well edited' (AU), 'pretentious jargon' (BR), 'program should include an introduction to ways of becoming a published author' (CA), and 'students have not learned to write cogently and succinctly' (US).

Inadequate emphasis on the familiarization with research methods is perceived to be a problem. Eleven responses were received on this issue and they included the comments, 'students would benefit from structured and coherent instruction in research methods early in their programme' (AU), 'choice and understanding of research methodology' (BR), 'not enough coursework on methodology' (CA), and 'exposure to a range of research methods and their relationship to outcomes' (US).

Long completion time for the thesis was an issue recorded eight times. Respondents stated problems existed with 'the minimum and maximum amount of time allowed for the thesis to be completed' (AU), 'lack of guidance on time' (BR), 'an inordinate amount of time is spent writing the thesis' (CA), and with the 'completion time permitted' (US).

Another perspective of this problem could be seen in the four responses that identified completion time for the entire doctoral programme as a problematic issue. This was identified through comments such as, 'ensuring that completion times are not excessive' (AU), 'three years maximum recommended' (BR), 'length of time taken to complete the requirements' (CA), and 'keep study within reasonable time limit' (US).

All the above issues were identified as problems in Australia, Britain, Canada and the United States. What follows are problematic issues recorded in at least three countries.

Except in Britain, the lack of an alternative to the traditional thesis was seen as a problem by 10 scholars. They said that 'students attempting PhDs in areas of study which do not have a research tradition or in interdisciplinary areas should not be expected to earn a degree by research only' (AU), 'options in lieu, e.g., a supervised practicum' (CA), and 'is the preparation of a dissertation a waste of time in fields where publication is in the form of short articles?' (US).

Part-time study is a problem for some of the scholars. It was identified eight times and comments received included, 'whether it is possible to complete part or all of the degree by correspondence (part-time) study' (AU), 'lack of opportunity to take courses part time' (CA), 'nature of research for part-time students' (US).

Overly long theses were mentioned eight times. Related comments included, 'theses are too long' (AU), 'many theses are unnecessarily long' (CA), and 'does a prescribed length only encourage irrelevance and bloated organization?' (US).

The availability of courses is a problem. Five scholars indicated that courses were not available and that this was 'particularly difficult for schools with small numbers of doctoral students' (AU), 'due to perception held by professors there are no rewards' (CA), and in 'conflict with other heavily subscribed courses' (US).

The following were deemed problems in one or two countries. Financial support to undertake the study for the doctoral degree and the related research was an issue identified 12 times in Canada and the United States. Respondents said there was 'inadequate financial support' (CA), and that 'available financial support controls areas of research' (US).

Interdisciplinary study and research is a problem according to five respondents. They said that there are 'difficulties in doing interdisciplinary research' (CA), and that there is 'insufficient interdisciplinary emphasis' (US).

Four comments associated with the lack of creativity were received. These comments were, 'conservative effects of the study component' (AU), 'novelty of the research is an important factor' (US), 'lack of self-directed research' (US), and 'traditional teaching does not force or allow the student to use creativity and or thinking skills' (US).

Problems associated with the acceptance and the non-acceptance of group or team thesis research was raised by four scholars. Two of them said there is a 'bias to large lab group research in many fields' (US), and that there is 'too much stress on individual research, too little provision for team research especially in the humanities and social sciences' (US).

The lack of practical commercial or industrial experience as part of the doctoral degree was identified as a problem three times. One scholar stated that 'in professional areas there should be some practicum associated with the PhD requirements' (CA), and another said 'practica are needed' (US).

With respect to languages two respondents believe a problem exists. In their words there is 'too little use of foreign languages as research tools' (US), and doctoral students need either 'linguistic or analytical skills' (US).

Two participants said that not incorporating teaching into the doctor of philosophy degree programme is a problematic issue. For them the doctorate fails 'to prepare undergraduate teachers' (US), and that students need to be 'exposed to formal experiences dealing with teaching in their disciplines and in higher education' (US).

Summation

As revealed briefly here the requirements for doctoral degrees, the acquisition of these degrees, and the subsequent activities of graduates are perturbing to many who ask questions about doctorates and their place in modern society. As internationalism and global economics exert their irresistible pressures, as universities struggle with budget allocations and increasing societal demands, as communication increases in speed and frequency, as knowledge expands explosively, and as special interest groups vie for political power, doctoral degrees can only reflect the resultant tensions.

Considering the contribution that holders of doctorates can make to educational institutions, to the gross national product of countries through scientific research and development work, and to the intellectual and cultural life of nations, and noting that the economic, educational and political realities of the future are international in scope, the responsibilities placed on future doctoral graduates will no doubt increase greatly.

In order to meet these new responsibilities satisfactorily, doctoral students will be required to study different subject matter, and to acquire knowledge in a manner dissimilar to contemporary practices (Carter, 1980; Cross, 1987; Weston, 1988b; Jacobson, 1989; MacGregor, 1991).

In a text prepared to assist students in completing their doctoral degrees,

Sternberg (1981: 5) states that the '. . . dissertation doctorate is certainly the least understood institution in American higher education.' It appears that all of the problems described above fall around Sternberg's rubric, and it would seem logical that his statement applies without fear of categorical denial to doctorates offered in Australia, Britain and Canada.

The doctoral degree has been in existence for over 800 years, and although aspects of it and the process of attaining it may be a serious concern and in need of restructuring, the doctorate is not going to lose its credibility quickly. Damning evidence, as produced by Anderson (1992) and Sykes (1988) to support their arguments that university professors have caused the demise of higher education, will probably not bring any quick changes even though changes certainly appear warranted. The emphasis on research that Smith (1990) and many others consider excessive and deleterious will be difficult to de-emphasize.

One factor frequently overlooked is the increasing body of knowledge and the increasing number of knowledge disseminators that doctoral students must search through and contend with.

As examples, with the figure for the previous year or compilation in parentheses, Salk (1992: vii) lists approximately 126,000 (116,000) different periodicals in 788 (668) subject areas; in the United States, Gravesande (1991: v) catalogues approximately, 1,000,000 (854,771) books in print from over 40,000 (33,000) publishers; in Britain, Whitaker (1992: v) indicates 529,250 (484,839) titles from 18,905 (16,168) publishers. The *Times Higher Education Supplement* (1993) records that, '(i)n the four years to 1991, the number of serial titles grew by 1,000 a month – it is now estimated that over 1 million science articles are published a year, which is 2,740 articles every day (Anderson, 1992: 82); and the *Directory of Electronic Journals, Newsletters and Academic Discussion Lists,* published by the Association of Research Libraries in the United States, contains 900 (627) entries in 1992, an increase of almost 45 per cent in one year. One forecast by the World Organization for the Future of Higher Education is that knowledge in some fields will increase by 100 per cent between the years 1990 and 2000 (Perica, 1990: 20).

Conclusion

From the literature, concerns about doctoral education are being expressed in Australia, Britain, Canada and the United States. More specifically, there are numerous and serious problems associated with doctoral degrees. These problems have existed for a considerable period of time. If they are left unresolved, they will no doubt be exacerbated by the unrelenting increase of scientific knowledge, by the demands placed on doctoral education by candidates and employers, and by the rapid national and international changes taking place around the globe.

4

Potential Solutions

The tragedy of all political action is that some problems have no solution.
(James Joll)

Most doctoral degrees share similar problems. International literature published between 1960 and 1991 reveals the existence of consistent problems with doctoral degrees. A comparison (triangulation) of this literature with the results of the PhD study revealed only three problematic issues, identified in the first phase of the study, which are not discussed in the literature; hence the issues were not incorporated into the second phase. These three issues are lack of practica, insufficient suitable courses and the need for foreign languages.

This similarity between the international literature and the findings of the PhD study demonstrates the credibility (validity) of problems related to the doctor of philosophy degree as being pertinent to doctoral degrees in general.

Of course, the following solutions which were posed, each with a seven-point Likert scale, in the PhD study, have limitations. Their potential is limited by several factors that impinge upon the application and the efficacy of each solution. These factors include the fundamental components of the doctorate, the acquisition process and the inertia inherent in the doctoral degree. No solution is perfect for every doctorate.

Doctoral degree components

The acquisition model of the traditional doctoral degree incorporates three fundamental components.

Lengthy study
The time doctoral students spend doing all those things, whether they be directed (e.g. attending courses) or non-directed (e.g. reading, thinking) that assist with the acquisition of the doctorate.

Original research
Research not previously undertaken, carried out in accordance with university regulations, with the approval of a department or faculty, and under the observation of an individual deemed qualified to monitor doctoral research.

Thesis preparation
The manuscript that documents the original research (some institutions use the term dissertation).

A number of programme solutions or actions related to these components will most likely have a positive impact on the resultant doctorate. The overall implications of these actions are described below, and this is followed by a discussion of the actions grouped specifically around each of the three components.

Programme solutions

Defining appropriate doctoral research
As a doctoral degree problem this issue has appeared consistently in the literature. Good examples can be found in Lynton and Elman (1987: 138–45), Storr (1973: 66–79) and Winfield *et al.* (1987: 11–18).

In the PhD study the majority of the respondents (75 per cent) were of the opinion that the potential solution 'insisting the priority of doctoral research is to add to knowledge' (i.e. original contribution), will help resolve a problem perceived to exist with the doctorate. Only four respondents (6 per cent) thought this action would have no effect.

To the proposed potential solution, 'insisting the priority of doctoral research is to enhance learning' (i.e. research training) the majority (63 per cent) believed the result on the doctorate would be positive. Approximately one quarter (27 per cent) of the replies were negative.

The potential solution 'insisting that doctoral research be "basic" or "pure", not "applied" or "practical"' prompted 51 (81 per cent) of the 63 respondents to indicate the action would have a negative impact on the doctorate, whereas only 11 (17 per cent) thought the impact would be positive.

Defining purpose of study/courses
From the literature this is not generally a concern in North America. For those countries (e.g. Australia, Britain) where course work is not tradition-ally part of a doctoral degree, a problem is said by some scholars to exist, specifically Ash *et al.* (1988: 2–4) and Stranks (1984). Clarifying the purpose of study or courses may be a potential solution to this doctoral degree problem.

As a solution posed in the PhD degree study, 'defining the reason for, the extent of and the method of mandatory/required study/courses' the prognosis was positive. An obvious majority (68 per cent) of the respondents indicated the doctorate would be improved by this action. Three replies (5 per cent) indicated a negative consequence would result, while the other 16 replies (27 per cent) indicated no effect.

Improving advising/directing/supervising
The need to improve the advising/directing/supervising of doctoral work has been documented in the literature for well over 30 years. Two good examples can be found in the Council of Graduate Schools (1990b: 6–8) and Moses (1984). As a potential solution to a doctoral degree problem it has been recommended in Australia, Britain, Canada and the United States.

In reply to the proposed solution, 'improving the advising, directing, or supervising of doctoral students', 39 respondents (60 per cent) indicated this action would most likely have a strong positive impact on the doctorate. The remaining respondents (40 per cent) indicated a weak or moderate positive effect would be the outcome. This solution is the only one for which no neutral or negative responses for the resultant doctorate were given in the PhD study.

Clarifying thesis standards
As a solution to problems perceived to exist with the doctoral thesis, this action has also been strongly recommended in the literature. Readers are referred to works by Cude (1987: 115–18), Grigg (1965: 53–69), and Spurr (1970: 132–3). Recently, a comprehensive document addressing this problematic issue has been published by the Association of American Universities (1990).

To the potential solution 'clarifying the standards for preparing and evaluating the doctoral thesis', proposed in the PhD study, one respondent (2 per cent) predicted a negative consequence, four (6 per cent) indicated no effect, and 57 (92 per cent) recorded a positive prognosis.

Requiring writing skills
Few references to poor or inadequate writing in doctoral theses can be found in the literature, apart from that in Berelson's (1960: 247, 248) work.

As a solution to the problem perceived to exist by the participants in the PhD study, 'requiring all doctoral students acquire writing skills before they write the thesis' produced an overall positive prediction. Only four panellists (6 per cent) indicated this action would have a negative result on the doctorate. Whereas 56 panellists (89 per cent) indicated a positive effect would be the outcome.

Ensuring financial support
Assisting doctoral candidates financially is considered a potential solution to a perceived problem. Although it appears infrequently in the literature, it is mentioned by Bladen (1962: 53), and more recently by the Association of American Universities (1990: 11, 17, 18).

To the statement, 'ensuring all doctoral students receive a stipend and/or funds to conduct their research' posed in the PhD study, 52 responses (84 per cent) produced a positive prediction for the resultant doctorate. Respondents who believed this action would have no effect on the doctorate totalled eight (13 per cent).

Increasing research methods study

The problematic need for doctoral students to study research methods is documented consistently in the literature (Ash *et al.*, 1988: 3, 4; Association of American Universities, 1990: 10).

Respondents in the PhD study reacted to the proposed solution, 'increasing the emphasis placed on the study of research methods' as follows. Eleven (17 per cent) of the respondents indicated the action would have no effect on the doctorate. Of the remaining respondents, 50 (79 per cent) believed the action would enhance the resultant doctorate, and two (3 per cent) indicated a negative result would occur.

Approving alternatives to thesis

A perceived problem within doctoral degree programmes, has resulted in the proposal of alternatives to the thesis as a solution. This issue has been documented in the literature emanating from Australia (Nightingale, 1984), Canada (Cude, 1987: 85, 86) and the United States (Lynton and Elman, 1987: 140).

In the PhD study, 'approving alternatives to the traditional thesis' (e.g. a book or journal articles), produced a pronounced difference in thoughts. Although almost half (46 per cent) of the respondents foresee the action having a negative impact, over one third (41 per cent) predicted a positive impact. Both the moderately negative effect and moderately positive effect garnered the most support, with over one quarter (27 per cent) and approximately a fifth (21 per cent) of the respondents supporting each respectively. Eight respondents (13 per cent) indicated the action would have no effect.

Decreasing time to complete thesis

Excessive time for the preparation of the thesis is a long-standing problem perceived to be associated with the doctoral degree. Time limitations have been discussed at length in the literature since the 1960s.

To the statement, 'decreasing the time allowed to write the thesis', a deleterious outcome was predicted by respondents in the PhD study. Only 17 of them (28 per cent) indicated the action would have a positive effect on the doctorate. Whereas 28 respondents (46 per cent) thought a negative outcome would occur, and of these, 13 (21 per cent) thought the outcome would be moderately or strongly negative. The remaining 16 respondents (26 per cent) were of the opinion that the action would have neither a positive nor a negative impact on the resultant degree.

Attainment through part-time studies

The issue of part-time study is not widely considered to be a problem in doctoral education. One early tangential reference to the issue can be found in the work of Swann (1968). Considering the recent increase in the number of part-time higher education students, part-time doctoral study will no doubt become a more prominent issue in the 1990s and beyond (Tight, 1990).

In the PhD study the respondents reacted favourably to the solution, 'permitting and facilitating the attainment of all components of the doctorate by part-time students'. This proposal resulted in 39 respondents (62 per cent) giving a positive answer, compared with 16 (25 per cent) who gave a negative answer. Eight respondents (13 per cent) thought there would be no effect on the programme.

Requiring shorter thesis

Another issue raised consistently in the literature is the overly long doctoral thesis. Interestingly, in the PhD study the proposed solution 'requiring the written thesis be shorter than the existing norm' (i.e. fewer pages), the largest group of scholars thought it would have no effect on the resultant degree. Twenty (32 per cent) were of this opinion. Of the remaining respondents, 24 (38 per cent) indicated one of the three positive effect rankings, and 19 (30 per cent) indicated one of the three negative rankings.

Approving interdisciplinary emphasis

The need for interdisciplinary activity is not described in the literature as a major problem with respect to doctoral degrees.

When the proposal 'approving interdisciplinary study' was made to the participants in the PhD study it produced a predominantly positive response (83 per cent). Only two respondents (3 per cent) thought the action would cause a negative effect on the programme.

Decreasing time to complete doctorate

As a problem perceived to exist with the doctoral degree, excessively long completion time appears often in the literature from all of the countries mentioned in this work. Within this literature, three and four years are frequently mentioned as desirable maximum periods for acquiring a doctoral degree.

For the proposal, 'decreasing the time allowed to complete all components of the doctorate' in the PhD study, the modal response was four (no effect), with 18 scholars (29 per cent) giving this answer. Of the remaining respondents, 27 (44 per cent) predicted a range of negative outcomes, and 17 (27 per cent) were of the opinion that decreasing the time would have a positive outcome.

Accepting creativity

This is another issue that appears in the literature of the four countries discussed. The literature recommends creative research and theses be accepted, which, it is believed, will improve doctoral degree programmes.

To the statement, 'accepting "creative" approaches to research' (i.e. novel in lieu of traditional approaches) posed in the PhD study, a majority of 34 respondents (55 per cent) believed the outcome of this action would be positive. At the other end of the continuum, 19 respondents (31 per cent) thought a negative situation would develop with respect to the doctorate.

Approving group research

Not until recently has the issue of group or collaborative research appeared in the literature (Association of American Universities, 1990: 24, 25; Sekhon, 1989; Swinnerton-Dyer *et al.*, 1982: 80, 81). As a proposed solution in the PhD study, 'approving group or team research' (i.e. thesis research conducted by more than one student) produced a somewhat balanced reaction. Seven (11 per cent) of the respondents indicated that this action would most likely have no effect on the degree. The remainder were almost equally split in their prognoses. Those who predicted a negative outcome (43 per cent) were outweighed slightly by those who predicted a positive result (46 per cent).

Incorporating teacher training

This proposed solution appears frequently in the North American literature (Boyer, 1990: 71; Curtis, 1985: 36; Smith *et al.*, 1991: 135, 136), but little mention of it is made elsewhere.

When those participating in the PhD study were asked about 'incorporating teacher training into the doctoral programme' (i.e. teaching doctoral students how to teach), 38 respondents (60 per cent) predicted a positive outcome; only 12 respondents (19 per cent) thought a negative effect would ensue.

Component Specific Actions

Some actions grouped around the *lengthy study* component could have a distinct positive effect on the traditional doctorate. These actions are as follows: defining the reason for, the extent of and the method of mandatory/required study/courses; improving the advising, directing or supervising of students; increasing the emphasis placed on the study of research methods; permitting and facilitating the attainment of all components of the doctorate by part-time students; approving interdisciplinary study; and incorporating teacher training into the doctoral programme. Turning to the negative projections, only decreasing the time allowed to complete all of the components was seen as possibly having a detrimental effect on the doctorate.

With respect to *original research* there was one action, approving group or team research, for which there was no meaningful difference between the number of study respondents who indicated a negative prognosis and those who indicated a positive prognosis for the resultant doctorate. This split in the response indicates a clear difference of opinions, and further research is needed before any action is implemented.

Two actions were seen by the respondents as most likely having a negative effect on original research. These actions were as follows: insisting that doctoral research be basic or pure, not applied or practical; and decreasing the time allowed to complete all components of the doctorate.

All of the remaining actions related to the fundamental component of original research were viewed positively. These actions include: insistence that the priority of doctoral research is to add to knowledge (i.e. original contribution); insisting that the priority of doctoral research is to enhance learning (research training); improving the advising, directing or supervising of doctoral students; ensuring all doctoral students receive a stipend and or funds to conduct their research; permitting and facilitating the attainment of all components of the degree by part-time students; approving interdisciplinary study; and, accepting creative approaches to research (i.e. novel in lieu of traditional approaches).

For the *thesis preparation* component two related actions were perceived to have a greater likelihood of causing a negative impact on the doctorate: decreasing the time allowed to write the thesis; and decreasing the time allowed to complete all components of the doctorate.

Positive predictions by the panel were associated with four actions. Specifically, improving the advising, directing or supervising of doctoral students; clarifying the standards for preparing and evaluating the doctoral thesis; requiring all doctoral students to acquire writing skills before they write their theses; and permitting and facilitating the attainment of all components of the doctorate by part-time students.

Two actions that a roughly equal number thought would produce either positive or negative effects are, approving alternatives to the traditional thesis (e.g. a book or journal articles), and requiring the written thesis be shorter than the existing norm. Note the former produced a pronounced divergence in the overall response, and the latter produced a no-effect response almost equal in size to the positive and negative effects.

Thus, corrective actions aimed at enhancing the traditional doctoral degree can be directed at all three of the fundamental components. The results of implementing these innovations should be beneficial if the positive prognostic projections of the study participants are noted, and the existing educational history, culture and infrastructure are taken into consideration.

But it needs to be remembered that the implementation of any action related to a component may not produce immediate results. Requiring all doctoral students to acquire writing skills before they write their theses, could stimulate an ongoing series of writing seminars that would not necessarily produce immediate improvement.

The process becomes more complex when an action flows across all three of the components. For example, improving the advising, directing, or supervising of doctoral students could necessitate an entirely new approach to a doctorate. Such an approach may take considerably more time, and certainly more co-ordination and co-operation if it is going to be applied across all of the components to improve the resultant degree.

Perhaps the most demanding situation would be one where several actions to improve a doctorate are implemented simultaneously. Looking at a scenario where only two actions are initiated it becomes apparent that some actions, when combined, could be counterproductive and may have a negative impact on the resultant doctorate. Approving group or team research might, because of newly-created problems related to communication and commuting, increase the time taken by candidates to complete their original research. This, in conjunction with decreasing the time allowed to complete all of the components, may result in a doctorate being completed in a time that exceeds the new officially desired completion time.

Summation

Numerous solutions have been proposed within the literature to rectify problems believed to exist with doctoral degrees, and a recent study of the doctor of philosophy degree has confirmed similar beliefs concerning related problems and actions/solutions that may resolve them (see Table 4.1).

With the exception of one solution related to student advisers/directors/supervisors, every proposed solution produced both positive and negative responses. There can be no doubt that there will be opponents to every substantive solution recommended to rectify problems with doctoral degrees. For wherever any educational programme exists, and especially one as old as the doctoral degree, there will be those who want to maintain the status quo.

Any proposal, if it is to be successfully implemented and adopted, must accommodate the inertia of the doctoral degree. But this inertia has both power and direction, which, in some circumstances may be intractable. On this point, Bowen and Rudenstine (1992: 55) describe how graduate programmes 'tend to take on lives of their own'. So it seems there will always be hurdles to overcome in the course of having doctoral programme related solutions successfully implemented and accepted in universities.

Table 4.1 International PhD study summary statistics

Proposed action solution	% Prognoses		
	Neg.	*No effect*	*Pos.*
Insisting the priority of doctoral research is to add to knowledge (i.e. original contribution).*	19	6	75
Insisting the priority of doctoral research is to enhance learning (i.e. research training).	27	10	63
Insisting doctoral research be 'basic' or 'pure' not 'applied' or 'practical'.	81	2	17
Defining the reason for, the extent of, and the method of mandatory/required study/courses.	5	27	68
Improving the advising, directing, or supervising of doctoral students.	0	0	100
Clarifying the standards for preparing and evaluating the doctoral thesis.	2	6	92
Requiring all doctoral students acquire writing skills before they write the thesis.	6	5	89
Ensuring all doctoral students receive a stipend and/or funds to conduct their research.	3	13	84
Increasing the emphasis placed on the study of research methods.	3	17	79
Approving alternatives to the traditional thesis (e.g. a book or journal articles).	46	13	41
Decreasing the time allowed to write the thesis.	46	26	28
Permitting and facilitating the attainment of all components of the doctorate by part-time students.	25	13	62
Requiring the written thesis be shorter than the existing norm (i.e. fewer pages).	30	32	38
Approving interdisciplinary study.	3	14	83
Decreasing the time allowed to complete all components of the doctorate.	44	29	27
Accepting 'creative' approaches to research (i.e. novel in lieu of traditional approaches).	31	15	55
Approving group or team research (i.e. thesis research conducted by more than one student).	43	11	46
Incorporating teacher training into the doctoral programme (i.e. teaching doctoral students how to teach).	19	21	60

* Number of scholars responding to each proposal, 60–63

Source: Noble (1992: 90–104)

Conclusion

The 18 solutions discussed above all involve modifying at least one of the three fundamental components of the doctoral degree (i.e. lengthy study, original research, thesis preparation). Emphasis in the PhD study was on amending the existing format of the doctorate, not on implementing radical innovations. In subsequent chapters, the implications of these solutions on four non-traditional doctoral degree programme formats are discussed and the associated implications for university administrators are raised.

5
Non-traditional Programmes

Non-traditional programs encourage diversity of individual opportunity.
(S. B. Gould)

Doctoral degrees have evolved slowly over centuries. Over time admend-
ments to the requirements for a doctorate have occurred (e.g. residency),
but the three fundamental components of the traditional degree remain
unchanged. All of the minor changes to the degree that have occurred
since its inception have been evolutionary, and more dramatic changes,
described here as revolutionary, are not recorded in the higher education
literature prior to relatively recent times.

What has now developed is the perception, in the minds of a number of
reformers, that traditional doctoral degree programmes, including those
offered in unconventional formats, no longer fulfil the academic and
professional needs of society, and that major changes are called for.

This perceived problem has prompted thinkers to deliberate on the
matter, and subsequently, several non-traditional doctoral degree programmes have been described and promoted in the higher education
literature published in Australia, Britain, Canada and the United States.
All of these non-traditional formats are revolutionary as they break from
long established precedent.

The detailed merits of these proposed programmes, and what exactly
has prompted them is not our concern here. Rather, the focus of attention
will be on the impact the proposed solutions described in the preceding
chapter will have on four non-traditional doctoral degree programmes.
These programmes are: Group Research, Three-Track, Time-Limited
and Two-Track.

Group-research programme

Stranks, who has studied the doctor of philosophy degree in Australia, has
considered several constraints on the doctorate as it exists in that country.
In addition to the problems of financial restrictions for students and a bleak

future for academic employment, Stranks discusses the process of socialization. This latter constraint is exacerbated by the fact that the majority of
the monitoring professors have limited research experience outside of the
university, which does not enable them to stimulate the student into
acquiring a rich array of research interests – 'if we are to enhance the
personal qualities of our postgraduates we should take steps to develop
greater diversity of interest within the postgraduate in all fields of scholarly
activity' (Stranks, 1984: 174).

He goes on to suggest that this undesirable situation may be overcome
through the introduction of group research in doctoral programmes, in all
disciplines it is assumed, and he claims that this non-traditional approach to
the doctorate would result in the following outcome:

> Our present PhD programmes, however, tend to encourage a conver-
> gence of interests in the postgraduate student. The PhD, when
> undertaken within a research group, as distinct from the traditional
> isolated experience, has the important merit of providing intellectual
> competitors. This would create benefit derived from peer group
> activity as distinct from the research supervisor's activity, and group
> work is also important in reducing the postgraduate's sense of
> isolation. Further, expanded group activity helps individual candi-
> dates understand the much broader aspects of their discipline.
>
> (Stranks, 1984: 174)

In Britain, this idea has been supported. Renouf (1989: 87) writes, 'that
at the root of poor completion rates and general dissatisfaction with PhD
research lie two problems: intellectual isolation, and an unrealistic and
poorly defined method of assessment – the thesis.' Centring his comments
around the social sciences doctorate, he states that for this doctoral degree a
new approach is called for. To Renouf, the solution is research undertaken
by a group of researchers, not just one researcher working alone. He
believes group research can be justified by at least three reasons which are
excerpted below:

> First, a PhD is currently an unrealistic piece of work because it requires
> a researcher to work alone on a topic which quickly achieves an
> overwhelming scale. Feelings of helplessness, inadequacy, an inability
> to cope, intellectual stagnation and confusion are common. These
> should not be considered as in some way inevitable or integral parts of
> the learning process. They are deeply counterproductive. A group
> PhD preserves the best parts of the 'traditional' PhD whilst overcoming
> the problem of isolation. Group project research allows for mutual
> development. It generates feedback and discussion. It provides a
> support network. It gives opportunities to work through theoretical
> problems, and it creates a realistic, collective working environment of
> the type found in all walks of life. Secondly, writing a thesis appears

more and more to be a test of stamina – a hellish rite of passage into the academic world. Difficulties are compounded by the implicit denial in a thesis of the developmental nature of PhD research, and the increasingly provisional nature of any conclusions reached, given the size of almost any research topic. Combining a series of reports with group project research creates a strong motivational framework. Reports validate the process of learning, as well as the end product of that process. And they recognize the provisional nature of research conclusions. Finally, there could be other advantages to group project work. If a project was considered worthy of further research, extra researchers could be added in. As some finished, others could take their place. Interdisciplinary research could be enhanced, with genuine debates and interaction between people with different disciplinary backgrounds required by the group structure.

(Renouf, 1989: 91)

What Renouf and Stranks claim is that the approach to learning how to undertake research, as it exists in traditional doctoral programmes, is not sufficiently effective. Both scholars believe a non-traditional approach would enhance the research learning process; both see group research as the appropriate innovative format.

Group research was addressed directly in the PhD study. In the initial phase of the study four respondents indicated that group research was a problem with respect to the doctorate. They said, depending on their point of view, that group research could be a problem because of its presence or its absence. One respondent said that there is 'bias to large lab group research in many fields', and another respondent said there is 'too much stress on individual research, too little provision for team research especially in the humanities and social sciences.'

The overall response to the proposed solution, 'approving group or team research' (i.e. thesis research conducted by more than one student), resulted in an almost balanced difference of opinion. Those who believed the outcome of approving group or team research would be negative (43 per cent), were numerically counterbalanced by those thinking the outcome on the resultant doctorate would be positive (46 per cent). This difference could mirror the existing situation in the physical sciences where group research is now a common occurrence.

To summarize: although all those who raised the problematic issue of group research in the PhD study were from the United States, Stranks writes about Australia and Renouf about Britain; as a problem the issue is certainly not restricted to one country; a compromise position would be one way of satisfying those of the more traditional persuasion; if group or team research was offered as an option for the fundamental component of original research, perhaps some doctoral students would have an alternative more compatible with their personal and academic needs.

Three-track programme

In a report prepared for university presidents, the future of post-secondary education was documented by several Canadian researchers. They claimed that 'the future development of graduate studies is the adaptability of graduate instruction to different fields of activity rather than one specific field' (Porter *et al.*, 1971: 99). They posed the question, are Canadian graduate schools producing the right product? This question was founded, in part, on Porter's earlier suggestion (1970) that the problem of Canadian graduates is their over-specialization. For Porter *et al.* (1971: 101), one conclusion they arrived at was that the doctor of philosophy degree 'may be out of date'.

As a way of overcoming this situation, Porter and his associates turned to the three-track degree format that has been proposed by Earle D. Nestmann a graduate student from York University, Canada, and Dr L. H. Cragg, the president of Mount Allison University, Canada. This proposal is succinctly summarized as follows:

> 1. Train some PhDs for undergraduate teaching (one quarter of the present PhDs in chemistry, they estimate, would go into this type of program); this section would not be heavily research oriented. 2. Train a second group in in-depth research; both research and course work would be broader than the present PhD programs. 3. Train the third group of PhD candidates around a core of courses with less specialization and more flexibility; out of this type of program would come leadership to overcome special technological problems such as pollution, planning for innovation, and industrial management including sales and market analysis.
>
> (Law, 1970: 31)

These three non-traditional options, which are recommended for the science disciplines, are seen by Porter *et al.* as viable and desirable alternatives to the traditional doctoral degree programme. Principally, what they suggest in their report is a doctorate that has three tracks or options – teaching, basic or pure research, applied or practical research. Insight into these three tracks can be achieved through an examination of two solutions that were posed in the PhD study.

For the solution relevant to teaching, the majority response was positive. Over 60 per cent predicted that a favourable outcome would most likely occur as a result of 'incorporating teacher training into the degree' (i.e. teaching doctoral students how to teach), whereas 19 per cent felt it would have a negative effect on the doctorate.

The second and third tracks are related to the original research-related solution, 'insisting that doctoral research be "basic" or "pure", not "applied" or "practical".' For this proposed solution a pronounced negative outcome would most likely occur according to the respondents. Eighty-one per cent of them foresee that insisting the research be basic/pure would result in a deleterious effect on the resultant doctorate. The opposite view was held by 17 per cent of the respondents.

To summarize: the results of the PhD study reveal there are supporters for all of the three tracks proposed by Porter and his colleagues; this three-track doctorate can accommodate conservatives and liberals, as it does not necessitate the total abandonment of the traditional doctoral programme format.

Time-limited programme

In Britain, the scholars Young, Fogarty and McRae (1987: 61) state that an influential number of academics believe 'it may not be possible to write a satisfactory doctoral dissertation in four years'. They also record that some administrators and policy-makers in higher education believe completing a doctoral degree in under four years is an attainable, and in fact desirable goal, for full-time students it is assumed.

What these scholars see is a bifurcation of views between those who see the doctorate as necessitating emphasis on a contribution to knowledge, and those who see the doctorate as being a research training process. Given this, Young, Fogarty and McRae suggest that the onus of proof lies with those who support the four-year limit. The task being one of demonstrating parity of esteem or equality between the traditional doctorate, which requires more than four years to complete, and the non-traditional doctorate, which would be completed in less than four years. For these authors parity of esteem can be achieved through time-limited study:

> One way forward might be to tackle the problem of parity of esteem together with the problem of over-long completion times. The solution to these linked problems may be found in time-limited study . . . a second route to the doctorate could be offered, based on the taught programme followed by a period of research culminating in a lesser thesis which, while it would represent a contribution, would be less substantial a contribution to knowledge than is customarily expected. A high completion rate would be secured by the requirement that the thesis be submitted no later than nine (or twelve) terms from registration. Parity of esteem would follow from the accomplishment of a respectable piece of work within a prescribed period of time . . . Thus there might exist two alternative modes of doctoral study – "Mode A" and "Mode B" . . . The second mode we see as time-limited and partly taught, and we see no reason why very high submission rates should not be obtained there. Successful completion in that mode could be reckoned to enjoy parity of esteem by virtue of its adherence to a fixed completion date.
>
> (Young, Fogarty and McRae, 1987: 61, 62)

This proposal is a revolutionary approach to the alleged problem of long completion times. Authors from several countries have studied this issue, and the most common question raised concerns itself with restructuring the traditional programme to facilitate completion within a time limit (Carnegie Commission on Higher Education, 1971: 31; Kerr, 1971: 28; Rudd, 1985: 134; Spurr, 1970: 138). Many in academe believe this to be a desirable goal.

What Young, Fogarty and McRae are suggesting, however, is a non-traditional mode to attain a doctoral degree, an optional mode that necessitates completion of the degree in a maximum of four years. It should be noted that completion time is a controversial issue in the United States, Canada and Australia as well as Britain. And, as highlighted in chapter three, universities in Britain are penalized if doctoral candidates take longer than four years to complete their doctorate.

As described, the underlying rationale for this proposed time-limit innovation is a difference in opinion in what constitutes the legitimate focus for a doctorate – should the focus be a contribution to knowledge, or should it be the training of researchers?

On both points, that is contributing to knowledge and training researchers, the majority of the scholars were affirmative. More specifically, to the proposed solutions 'insisting the priority of doctoral research is to add to knowledge' (i.e. original contribution) and 'insisting the priority of doctoral research is to enhance learning' (i.e. research training), the respondents predicted a positive outcome would most likely occur. For the first action the response was over 75 per cent, and for the second approximately 63 per cent. This is interpreted to mean that as foci both are valued and desired. Similar findings are discussed by Winfield *et al.* (1987: 12). In addition, these responses underscore the rationale described by Young, Fogarty and McRae.

Turning to their proposed innovation, the time-limited doctorate, three solutions suggested to the panel help clarify the issue of the time variable. With respect to the issue of long completion times taken for the thesis, one respondent said that 'an inordinate amount of time is spent writing the thesis.' On the issue of too lengthy theses the comment 'a prescribed length only encourages irrelevance and bloated organization' was offered. Concerning the time taken to complete the entire degree, one respondent thought a problem existed with the 'length of time taken to complete the requirements'.

To address these problems three solutions were posed in the PhD study: 'decreasing the time allowed to write the thesis', 'requiring the written thesis be shorter than the existing norm' (i.e. fewer pages), and 'decreasing the time allowed to complete all components of the doctorate'. For the first and third solutions the majority of responses were negative, 46 and 44 per cent respectively, and for the second 38 per cent of the respondents were positive.

To summarize: the respondents were in favour of reducing the size of the thesis, but not in favour of limiting the time to complete the written thesis or the overall programme; a time-limited degree may not result in an improved doctoral degree.

Two-track programme

Following on the heels of several earlier papers (Andersen, 1983; Crosson and Nelson, 1986; Dill and Morrison, 1985), which compared the requirements of different doctorates, another author has left an imprint in this area of study. What he proposes is a two-track doctor of philosophy degree.

Courtenay (1988) states that his proposal is related specifically to the discipline of education. He sees the need for it as a way to deal with the issue of distinction and thereby reduce the confusion over the two doctorates, that is the doctor of philosophy and the doctor of education. He states:

> The suggestion is made here that the various fields of education use the PhD only, but with two tracks, one for scholars of practice and one for scholarly practitioners. Several reasons appear to support that conclusion. In the first place, the PhD degree is well-known and understood by colleagues in the traditional disciplines, generally, and more specifically, by members of Graduate School program review committees. Some education faculty in all fields would criticize this reason as capitulation to external influential forces. Such criticism may be countered with two arguments. First, if it doesn't really matter what you call the degree, then why not choose the PhD? Secondly, if education faculty can communicate clearer to colleagues about the field of education by choosing the PhD label, then why not? . . . This solution is a 'viable' means because it promotes the end without restraining the flexibility that exists in doctoral education programs now. By having two PhD tracks, one for researchers/professors and one for administrators/teachers, the preference of the student and the two basic career objectives are met. Finally, this solution appears to be appropriate because it provides long-range benefits. Adopting a single degree with two tracks cause faculty to reflect more carefully about the content of departmental programs and the relevance of that content to the goals of the students . . . The PhD degree with two tracks would appear to be the viable solution for graduate programs in education. It communicates to other disciplines; it is flexible; and most importantly, it meets the needs of students.
>
> (Courtenay, 1988: 18, 19)

Twenty years earlier, Nichols (1967) also proposed a two-track doctoral degree programme. Founded on a research/teaching dichotomy, or as Nichols labelled it an honours/pass differentiation, he claims there is a need to acknowledge the two purposes of the doctorate. By acknowledging these purposes Nichols believes it is possible to create two doctoral degrees, each of which would equip graduates to undertake their primary function in professional life – either to conduct research or to teach; a belief shared and expressed by Anderson (1992: 78).

For Nichols, the honours doctor of philosophy degree would include periods of independent study, seminar courses, research training and a piece of original research work all undertaken in four years. The pass doctorate would place emphasis on interpretation and synthesis, would include supervised teaching experience, seminars on writing with the intent of having journal articles published, all of which would be achieved within a maximum of four years. Nichols (1967: 333) claims innovation is required because the existing doctoral programme 'hampers the creative (honours) and it can discourage the diligent (pass).'

An honours designation has recently been suggested as a worthwhile appellation for the doctor of philosophy degree in Britain. Ash *et al.* (1988) believe this doctorate should be awarded with distinction to those whose work is of particular merit. Although both Nichols and Courtenay suggest two degrees based on different programme orientations, and Ash and his associates suggest two diplomas based on merit, they all have a common point. They see a need to separate either the candidates or the graduates into two identifiable categories. Although one recommendation refers to a programme, and the other to an acknowledgement of a graduate's superiority, the two-track concept can be identified. Clearly, this is a non-traditional approach to a degree, for which historically there has only been one method of attainment and recognition.

Both of Nichols' honours and pass degrees raise three issues that need to be considered. One of these, that of completion time (within four years) is common, and the reader is directed back to the time-limited non-traditional doctorate where this issue is discussed. It suffices to say here that the respondents in the PhD study did not place time limitations in high stead.

For the honours doctorate, research training was identified as the second issue and it was also a solution posed to the panel. The proposed solution 'insisting the priority of doctoral research is to enhance learning' (i.e. research training) produced a majority positive response. The third issue deals with original research. When asked, what effect 'insisting the priority of doctoral research is to add to knowledge' (i.e. original contribution) would most likely have on the PhD degree, most respondents (63 per cent) answered positively.

For the pass doctorate a supervised teaching experience is the second issue. Looking at the action 'incorporating teacher training into the degree' (i.e. teaching doctoral students how to teach), the majority of the respondents (60 per cent) believed the outcome would be positive. Writing seminars was the third issue. Proposing the solution, 'requiring doctoral students acquire writing skills before they write their theses' produced an extremely positive response (89 per cent) from the scholars.

To summarise: as a non-traditional programme a two-track doctoral degree encourages a diversity of individual opportunity, unlike the restrictive traditional programme; this diversity also appears in the proposal to provide two forms of doctoral degree recognition; by providing this diversity, universities could possibly assist individuals to achieve a doctorate more compatible with their own individual needs and abilities.

Conclusion

At all times it must be borne in mind that doctoral degrees are not completely homogeneous. Although they have the same fundamental components, every country and every institution has its own historical traditions, and each demands additional elements that ensure heterogeneity. Making international comparisons of doctoral programmes, with the intent of identifying solutions to solve problems, always necessitates giving considerable attention to national and institutional differences. Clearly, there are several non-traditional formats that are revolutionary proposals to improve the doctoral degree. But implementing revolutionary change is always fraught with difficulties, and more modest recommendations may have more chance of being implemented successfully.

6

Administration

Administrators cannot order change in a college or university.
(Robert C. Nordvall)

Changing the status quo is possible. Doctoral degrees can be improved through the implementation of solutions that will act upon known problems. But to implement these positive actions requires administrative changes in traditional procedures, and administrators need the 'active participation of the faculty who carry out graduate education' (Association of American Universities, 1990: 4).

In higher education such changes or actions are commonly termed innovations in the literature (Seymour, 1988), and Good (1973: 302) defines them as 'the introduction of a new idea, method, or device in curriculum, educational administration, etc.' Higher education being an all encompassing term used here to describe the parts, procedures and products of post-secondary education.

As a backdrop, administrators need to remember the three motives for higher education: curiosity, utility and virtue, motives that have received different emphasis from students over the years (Hesseling, 1986: 121). Each of these motives demands unique application and assessment considerations, and each results in different implications for administrators.

Administrative implications

Administrators have many implications to consider when working with innovations implemented to resolve doctoral degree related problems. Here, administrators are defined as staff whose primary professional function is institutional governance. The term includes those whose positions are full time and salaried (e.g. department heads, faculty deans, presidents, registrars, vice-chancellors, etc.) as well as those whose positions are managerial and paid by honoraria (e.g. members of board of governors, members of senate, regents, etc.). We must note that most academic staff perform administrative functions, and that no changes in policy or procedure can be demanded by administrators in higher education (Seymour, 1987: 37).

With respect to implementing an innovation to improve the doctoral degree, administrators need to consider the fundamental components of the degree. From the cited PhD study, it is apparent that several actions will influence the procedures associated with these components, but that some of these actions are not likely to improve the doctorate. These actions, which have been grouped using the criterion of less than 30 per cent of the respondents in the PhD study predicting a positive effect on the doctorate, are discussed below (see Table 6.1).

By using 30 per cent of the response as the cut-off figure, an administrator knows that the most likely outcome of the actions in Table 6.1 would be negative (or no effect). Administrators might improve existing doctoral degree programmes, if they avoid incorporating the three actions listed in this table in their plans. Interestingly, the actions are not concentrated around any one fundamental component.

Actions that will most likely improve the resultant doctorate, are greater in number. These actions are the ones for which less than 30 per cent of the panel predicted negative effects (see Table 6.2). Initiating innovations based on these actions should allow administrators to improve the doctorate with a low risk of failure. Provided of course that all, or at least the most significant, ramifications that will inevitably occur as a result of the innovation have been predicted and planned for.

Of particular note among these 12 proposed actions is improving the advising, directing or supervising of doctoral students. This proposal was the only one to produce a unanimous response. All of the respondents to this question indicated that the outcome for the doctorate would most probably be positive.

Although not as pronounced, the responses to the proposed actions, requiring students/candidates to acquire writing skills before writing their theses and clarifying the standards for preparing and evaluating the

Table 6.1 Negative effect actions/solutions

Proposed action/solution	% Prognoses		
	Neg.	No effect	Pos.
Insisting that doctoral research be 'basic' or 'pure' not 'applied' or 'practical'.*	81	2	17
Decreasing the time allowed to write the thesis.	46	26	28
Decreasing the time allowed to complete all components of the doctorate.	44	29	27

* Number of scholars responding to each proposal, 60–63

Source: Noble (1992: 130)

Table 6.2   Positive effect actions/solutions

Proposed action/solution	% Prognoses		
	Neg.	*No effect*	*Pos.*
Insisting the priority of doctoral research is to add to knowledge (i.e. original contribution).*	19	6	75
Insisting the priority of doctoral research is to enhance learning (i.e. research training).	27	10	63
Defining the reason for, the extent of, and the method of mandatory/required study/courses.	5	27	68
Improving the advising, directing, or supervising of doctoral students.	0	0	100
Clarifying the standards for preparing and evaluating the doctoral thesis.	2	6	92
Requiring all doctoral students acquire writing skills before they write the thesis.	6	5	89
Ensuring all doctoral students receive a stipend and/or funds to conduct their research.	3	13	84
Increasing the emphasis placed on the study of research methods.	3	17	79
Permitting and facilitating the attainment of all components of the doctorate by part-time students.	25	13	62
Approving interdisciplinary study.	3	14	83
Accepting 'creative' approaches to research (i.e. novel in lieu of traditional approaches).	31	15	55
Incorporating teacher training into the doctoral programme (i.e. teaching doctoral students how to teach).	19	21	60

* Number of scholars responding to each proposal, 60–63

Source: Noble (1992: 132)

doctoral thesis, were similar and very favourable for the resultant doctorate. For these actions the positive responses from the scholars were 89 and 92 per cent respectively.

One cannot help but ask the question, what would be the outcome if administrators set about implementing these two actions within a doctoral degree programme? The associated costs are minimal, and none of the components of the doctorate would be manipulated so extensively that firm beliefs and practices would be severely compromised. Theses, written with well-developed writing skills, guided by clearly defined criteria, and evaluated against well-clarified standards could be a very promising and inexpensive objective for administrators involved with doctoral degrees.

Table 6.3   Ambiguous effect actions/solutions

Proposed action/solution	% Prognoses		
	Neg.	*No effect*	*Pos.*
Approving alternatives to the traditional thesis (e.g. a book or journal articles).*	47	13	41
Requiring the written thesis be shorter than the existing norm (i.e. fewer pages).	30	32	38
Approving group or team research (i.e. thesis research conducted by more than one student).	43	11	46

* Number of scholars responding to each proposal, 60–63

Source: Noble (1992: 133)

Advising/directing/supervising of doctoral students appears to be an ongoing institutional concern. As raised in chapter three, time to complete the doctorate is believed to be related to the quality of the adviser–advisee relationship. However, this relationship is not always perceived as the critical acquisition factor, as inadequate finances could be the biggest barrier to the timely completion of the thesis according to a recent report published by the Council of Graduate Schools (1991: 17).

Of the 18 actions proposed in the PhD study, three produced responses that were ambiguous, neither clearly negative nor positive, in their perceived impact on the doctorate (see Table 6.3). The action concerned with approving alternatives to the traditional thesis produced a response with almost balanced positive and negative predictions. A similar outcome prevailed for the action of approving group or team research. What may be important here for administrators is the fact that both actions are in tune with contemporary developments. Within some science disciplines alternatives to the traditional doctoral thesis are now permissible (e.g. compilation of related published papers, unofficially referred to as stapling), and group or team research is now a reality.

This cleft in the overall response probably represents a difference between the physical science disciplines, where group research is practised, and those other disciplines where collaborative research is not undertaken. Administrators need discipline-specific data if they are to make well-founded decisions for an associated doctoral programme; generalizing from one discipline to another would be the wrong thing to do.

The third ambiguous response was stimulated by the action related to the hypothetical requirement that theses be shorter. For this proposal the response was without any strongly pronounced most likely outcome, with the negative effect, no effect, and the positive effect all receiving over 30 per cent of the total response. It seems little will be gained by having a shorter thesis approved. Those scholars in favour of such action may well be counterbalanced by those not in favour, because it will, they believe, have a negative effect on the resultant doctoral degree.

Looking at the traditional doctoral degree, there are a number of innovations that could be taken, and which it has been predicted would improve the resultant doctorate. As pointed out, any movement in this direction necessitates serious attention being given by university administrators to the existing educational culture, history and infrastructure; failure to do so would demonstrate incompetence.

In addition, this attention must be international as well as national in perspective. To ensure reciprocity a doctoral degree programme must have an academic standing on a par with commonly accepted international and national norms. Care also needs to be exercised when considering actions/solutions that may be counterproductive if they are implemented simultaneously.

Turning to non-traditional doctorates, similar and dissimilar demands are placed on administrators. Similar in the sense that evolutionary changes (e.g. approving a shorter thesis) may be initiated in both traditional and non-traditional programmes, but certainly dissimilar in the sense that revolutionary changes (e.g. approving a two-track programme) will be associated with non-traditional doctoral programmes. A number of these programmes are described in the literature, and several have characteristics that correspond with proposed solutions that have been assessed favourably by the scholars of the PhD study.

Compensatory mechanisms

Considering the many parties involved in contemporary higher education (politicians, professional organizations, professors, proprietary interests, the public, etc.), administrators will inevitably be pressured during and after their involvement with the implementation of any innovation related to a doctoral degree. To eliminate or at best reduce this pressure, they need to anticipate and act on those aspects that influence the implementation of innovations, and to incorporate compensatory mechanisms that will neutralize negative resultant effects.

From Table 6.1 it can be seen that the solutions are restrictive, and administrators might do well to investigate some compensatory mechanism if one of these solutions must be initiated. For example, an innovation to improve the degree that decreases the time allowed to write the thesis will have more chance of being successful if the requirements associated with the thesis have been reduced, or restructured, to allow for the loss in available time (e.g. approving shorter more selective literature reviews).

Without this necessary compensation the innovation will most likely have a negative impact on the resultant degree. The Association of American Universities (1990: 4) is quite clear in its advice to administrators who are attempting to improve doctoral programmes: 'The task for university administrators responsible for doctoral education is to identify those (negative) contributory factors over which we can exert control and to adopt policies that will minimize their impact.'

Part-time study

One aspect of higher education that administrators have had to give more attention to over the last decade is part-time study (Noble, 1989; Smith and Saunders, 1991). For many reasons, students are undertaking their studies part time, breaking from the traditional full-time approach. For some programmes in some universities the number of part-time students now exceeds the full-time number. Inevitably, this development has also occurred in doctoral degree programmes. It is certainly not an uncommon occurrence in Britain, particularly in the social sciences, and the increasing time to graduate in the United States probably reflects this increase in part-time students (see Table 3.1).

As the PhD study revealed, a part-time approach to doctoral study does give cause for concern. For some faculty members a part-time approach to academic study can have several negative aspects. To these academics, 25 per cent in the PhD study, part-time study may suggest a lack of sincerity and dedication, or it may portend failure to graduate due to the inability of students to conclude their doctoral research or to complete the writing of their thesis. As many academics have seen themselves, a doctoral programme may be abandoned because of the travails of life that may not have been so acute if the doctoral programme had been brought successfully to a quicker conclusion.

Regardless, the trend to part-time study will continue. Administrators considering innovations related to doctoral degrees must give consideration to these types of student and accommodate them in their proposals. Tight (1993) has pointed out that in addition to the important distinction between, and the special needs associated with, part-time and full-time students, differences in student motives are significant. It is important for administrators, and of course academics, to appreciate whether a student is undertaking a doctoral programme for employment purposes (utility) or purely for reasons of personal interest (curiosity). The resultant difference in the focus, energy and intellectual endeavours between students can be great, and of course this difference will manifest itself regardless of whether students are full or part time.

International perspective

For administrators involved with doctoral degree programmes and any innovations related to these programmes one thing that cannot be disregarded is an international perspective. In an age of instantaneous communications, supersonic travel and problems without borders, an international perspective is paramount if a university wants to survive.

Although doctoral degree programmes can have different purposes in different countries, and although doctoral degree recipients can be involved in dissimilar work in different countries, there are numerous common purposes. It is these common international purposes that administrators ought to keep in mind when considering doctoral degree innovations. Not to do so will result in programmes having a limited national focus, which Winfield *et al.* (1987: 13) have commented on, and which, over time, devalues the international currency of the doctorate.

Conclusion

Numerous possible changes and non-traditional doctoral degree programme formats have been described in the literature. In one international study, 18 solutions related to doctoral degree problems were proposed and assessed, and not all were viewed favourably. Those involved with university administration appear to have a range of solutions to overcome doctoral degree problems, but closer examination shows up limitations in application and efficacy. Administrators have to remember the need for compensatory mechanisms in certain circumstances related to innovations, and the requirements for part-time study that is a growing aspect of doctoral degree programmes.

7

Recommendations

Every advance in education is made over the dead bodies of 10,000 resisting professors.
                    (Robert M. Hutchins, quoted by W. W. Jellema)

Recommendations are easy to make, but those leading to successful amendments in doctoral programmes are another matter. By observing existing programmes and perusing the literature, certain consistencies become apparent, and by adding these consistencies to the findings of the PhD study, some achievable recommendations can be arrived at. When considering these recommendations, seven of which are described in this chapter, readers are reminded to retain their international perspective.

In every doctoral degree programme there are potentially six major stakeholders. They are, the student/candidate, the adviser/director/ supervisor, the discipline, the university, the government/funding agency and the final employer. It is far beyond the intent of this small book to address every improvement that is best suited to these stakeholders in all situations. The recommendations made in this chapter are phylogenic and it is argued here they have international application. Doctoral degree related policies arising from student needs, national objectives, institutional purposes, the tradition of disciplines and employer demands must be derived from more specific, ontogenic research data, together with a detailed history of each doctoral programme.

Observations

In physics, inertia is the tendency of a body to maintain its present state of motion. In education, inertia is also at work and educational programmes have a strong tendency to continue in their current format and direction. The doctoral degree was first recorded at the university in Paris *circa* 1150, and since then it has developed an acquisition process and momentum that cannot be denied or dissipated quickly. With over eight centuries behind it the inertia associated with the doctoral degree is considerable, and it is the most profound and pervasive aspect of this degree to appreciate.

Different countries have different histories, different institutions have different policies and different departments have different foci related to doctoral degrees, but above all this are the indisputable, and up until now inviolate, components of the doctorate that must be completed before it can be acquired. The basic acquisition model of the doctorate incorporates the three universal and fundamental components of lengthy study, original research and thesis preparation.

No one acquires a doctoral degree from a reputable university without first engaging in some form of lengthy study (which may or may not include courses), without undertaking some form of original research (which in the physical sciences, may be group research), and without presenting research findings in some form of thesis (which may consist of several short documents joined into one manuscript). Although associated requirements may vary (e.g. residency), the completion of three fundamental components constitutes the model of the acquisition process of the doctoral degree.

Another characteristic of the doctoral degree is the fact it is a research qualification. The need for research generally goes undisputed, although the exact meaning of words such as independent, original and significant associated with research findings have never been defined to the satisfaction of all because they necessitate subjective interpretation. As an Australian scholar wrote, '(t)he standards by which theses are to be judged are incredibly vague'. Some of the many descriptions of these terms are described for the reader in Appendix F.

Finally, the doctoral degree is recognized internationally. Holders of a doctorate participate in international gatherings, and publish research findings in international journals, which subsequently are used to solve international problems. It is one of the few academic qualifications that crosses national borders without suffering devaluation, and in the age in which we live this hard international currency is extremely valuable.

Recommendations

What, if anything, needs to be done or can be done to improve doctoral degree programmes? We have a degree that has been in existence for over 800 years, a degree that necessitates the completion of three fundamental components and that has a research focus. We have numerous writers pointing out problems and possibilities for improvement; some of which must be legitimate, based on the frequency and distribution of the literature. Unfortunately, there is no sage to consult, and it would be unethical to involve doctoral students, unknowingly or unwillingly, in experimental programmes.

In any personal relationship, which is exactly what a student enters into with a doctoral adviser/director/supervisor, the normal vicissitudes of human life occur (Plowright, 1991), and as in any relationship things are not always harmonious. Within the context of higher education with all its complexities and demands, it is inevitable that personal and doctoral programme difficulties will arise. Addressing this point in a review of the literature, Hockey (1991) states, '(f)or the student to become an effective researcher there must be a movement from dependence and guidance to autonomy and colleagueship'.

Nevertheless, it is contended that some reforms in the doctoral degree attainment process are necessary and possible, and that these reforms will only be successful when amendments to the process do not depart greatly from current practices, because the inertia inherent in doctoral programmes cannot be circumvented. To ignore inertia will ensure the failure of well-intentioned reforms, certainly in traditional higher education institutions. With this in mind, and based on the PhD study and the literature, seven international recommendations follow:

1 Fewer students should be accepted into doctoral programmes, and those admitted should have an extremely sound master degree. This degree must have required course work in research methodology and the preparation of a major qualifying paper or master dissertation. By reducing the number, the better doctoral students will have more opportunity to get the professorial attention they deserve; time need not be spent on course work; and attrition, of overtaxed and overtaxing students, will be reduced. Some will say this is elitism, but the number of graduates should be roughly the same. (In his work Pelikan (1983: 67–77) discusses this elitism–egalitarianism issue.) What it would do is improve the environment for better doctoral students, and reduce the number of those who experience years of futile endeavours and anguish.

Several authors have written about the inadequacy of undergraduate education as a preparation to undertake a doctoral degree programme (Phillips and Pugh, 1987: 62; Turner, 1988), and Wright and Lodwick (1989) point out that young students, those who have completed only a baccalaureate degree, are often immature and lack the confidence to work well at the doctoral level.

With a good master degree, students will be more mature and the primarily North American requirement of course work would be reduced or made unnecessary. A scholar from the United States wrote, '(i)t is my opinion that too little emphasis is placed on research. The PhD degree has moved more toward course requirements'; and an Australian scholar stated, '(w)here coursework has been proposed as a required element, it has been attacked as lowering the standard of the degree, which is a *research* [scholar's italics] degree.'

In medicine the requirements for entry into degree programmes for physicians are extremely stringent, but once accepted into a programme, consistent hard work by a medical student almost in all cases guarantees graduation. Bowen and Rudenstine (1992: 108–9) give examples of medical school completion rates of 95 to 97 per cent. Unfortunately, doctoral degree programmes frequently operate in a reverse fashion. For most programmes it is somewhat easy to gain entry, but it is usually quite difficult to graduate; certainly to graduate in three to four years, especially in the humanities. It is not difficult to find evidence of this.

Doctoral programme attrition rates of over 50 per cent may exist in some disciplines; the exact figures are unknown because relevant statistics are not compiled, or if they are they are not made public. Few in academe can say they do not know or have not heard of individuals who had the potential but who were condemned to wander the nether world of abandoned doctoral students. Surely the system that allows excess and unsuited students into doctoral programmes is at fault – not the students/candidates who are often criticized for the predicament in which they find themselves (the blame-the-victim syndrome).

As staff shortages for some disciplines in some countries appear imminent, actions that reduce the time-to-degree are positive. And for universities receiving government funds based on enrolment, it would be more appropriate for financial support to be linked to a conferred doctoral degree. This would be easy to execute, and it would certainly be a more honest educational incentive than receiving monies for students who never graduate.

2 Because '(a) major problem for any graduate student is finding personal financial support', as a Canadian scholar points out, and because the Council of Graduate Schools (1991: 17) found inadequate financial support the most frequently cited barrier to completing the thesis, it is recommended that all non-affiliated doctoral students be employed and be paid the full base academic salary until graduation. Here non-affiliated means not receiving a salary, subsidy or leave of absence from any other institution.

To justify their small but adequate salary, doctoral students would have limited commitments to teach or assist with professorial research. Because the former can require excessive time, and because not all recipients of a doctoral degree intend to teach, the latter may be the most useful. Students would be exposed to research other than their own, and it would provide opportunities for them to assist with academic writing. Commenting on doctoral theses, a British scholar believes there is a '(t)endency to write, at excessive lengths, in a pretentious jargon'. Writing academic works should only improve theses.

Salaries paid to doctoral students would be offset by the work they provided and by halting all other forms of financial aid (e.g. assistantships). Reducing the number of students entering doctoral programmes would also help keep salary budgets low.

This recommendation has its foundation in functionalism; not all graduates choose to work in higher education or involve themselves with research once they complete their studies, but the majority do. Of course, students who must study part-time, for other than financial reasons, should also be accommodated. But the demands of doctoral degree programmes, the economy of the times, and the subsequent employment of graduates justifies full-time financial assistance.

3 One aspect of doctoral degrees that is frequently said to be a problem area is the relationship between the adviser (professor) and the advisee (student/candidate). As has been pointed out, this is a very human relationship, subject to all the joy and jubilation as well as the angst and aggravation that human relationships entail. No doubt there is always scope for improvement in these relationships, but regulations and policies can never guarantee continuous interpersonal harmony and substantive learning.

Many relationship problems might be prevented if both parties entered into a contract more as equals, as Wright and Lodwick (1989) were advised, each with a thorough knowledge of the other's doctoral degree perspective. Contracts are legally binding documents, which means both parties would have some protection in the event of a breakdown in the relationship. As it stands now, the student/candidate is, as Welford (1991: 18) points out, in a powerless and thus very vulnerable position. A written contract is recommended and an example is provided in Appendix G.

4 In those universities where it is still retained, the oral defence of the thesis should be dropped as an examination requirement for a doctorate. This practice, the *viva voce* or *rigorosum*, is an anachronism that can be traced back to the Middle Ages. In a chapter of his work on medieval universities, Schachner (1962: 326, 327) describes how the disputation was an integral part of doctoral student life, partly resulting from the fact that '(e)ach manuscript had to be laboriously copied on expensive parchment', but primarily due to religious imperatives.

Over time however, the handwritten thesis, the typed thesis, the word-processed thesis and now the laser-printed thesis have evolved. Today, examiners/readers assess 'hardcopy' doctoral theses. Where once no complete written document existed, at least until after the defence, and a verbal explanation and justification of the thesis was necessary, now multiple printed copies of the thesis are circulated and examined. For a considerable period of time, the presentation and the examination of doctoral theses has been done on paper.

At best, the oral defence can only repeat what the doctoral candidate has already written in the thesis. It can be a good forum for those with public speaking skills who are confident and who can think on their feet, all of which has nothing to do with a doctoral programme or subsequent employment. At worst, it provides an opportunity for thesis examiners to demonstrate their brilliance and ability to find fault in the thesis. For those candidates who do not possess a strong, confident voice and personality, plus the ability to parry verbal slings in a most sensitive way the experience can be disastrous.

Oral defences are outmoded, as many graduate deans told Berelson

(1960: 199–201) over 30 years ago. Procedurally, the defence is an imbalanced and therefore unjust process, because the candidate needs the approval of that examiner who may be opposed to the thesis. Examiners can, and do, enter bitter and rancorous disputes over doctoral research, and this type of development always leaves candidates helpless and in an extreme state of stress.

It is not uncommon for candidates to have their graduation delayed because of examiners who have entered into a dispute that someone within the university with some influence must diplomatically try to resolve. Few people can imagine the anxiety experienced by candidates in these cases as their lives, academic and personal, are held in abeyance.

Even worse, are those situations where candidates have been denied a doctorate because of their inability to defend their thesis. A Canadian scholar wrote, '(s)tudents should not be allowed to proceed to the point of starting a thesis or be allowed to engage in all the research and writing involved and then be turned back. The thesis defence should not be an opportunity to "weed out" students.'

At one time the oral defence of a thesis was necessary as it was the only way an argument could be publicly presented and justified (particularly to the clergy). But those days are long gone. Oral defences are now an unnecessary drain on doctoral candidates, thesis examiners and the financial resources of universities. They achieve nothing that is not already documented on paper by the candidates and the examiners. Glibness should not be equated with scholarliness.

The important issue is the examination of the thesis. Abolishing the thesis would go against the inertia associated with the doctorate, whereas dropping the oral defence does not lessen the thesis or its examination on paper. It would rightly put more emphasis on the examination of the written thesis and de-emphasize oral and visual presentation skills.

5 Traditionally, a number of academics examine the completed doctoral thesis; the exact number, including the thesis adviser/director/supervisor, is based on precedent (e.g. two or three in Britain, four to eight in North America) and the perceived complexity of the work. Usually, there is at least one external examiner, and as the role of external examiners is to ensure academic integrity, their services must always be retained.

However, one aspect of the thesis examination process that needs to be abolished is the requirement of examiner unanimity. Undertaking the necessary study and research, and writing the thesis to document that research always takes several years. Candidates who have had a research proposal approved, who have conducted the research, and who have written a thesis with professorial advice should not be denied a doctorate because of a negative examination report. On this point Ferber (1960) writes that such a case was brought to his attention, a case where 'the student had still not received his degree 11 years after he submitted his dissertation!'

We should not deceive ourselves that circumstances have improved since the 1950s and 1960s. Anderson (1992: 70) says the potential for abuse still exists today, and that it is 'awesome'.

A system of assessment that accepts at least one negative vote, a system similar to that which has existed in the past (Davinson, 1977: 17), needs to be re-adopted. This would prevent a candidate's career from being destroyed because of a disagreement between examiners. If there is only one external examiner and that person dissents, for reasons not related to integrity, a second external examiner should be consulted.

Because examiners can and do disagree, over personal points of view, professional perspectives and academic matters, is not sufficient reason to penalize doctoral candidates. Once a thesis is completed it may require *minor* improvements, most do. But a thesis should never be rejected or substantially rewritten because of one negative opinion. By not demanding unanimity, the thesis examination becomes an education, not an execution.

6 As previously stated, doctoral degrees are international, and as such, holders have a valid academic passport. Amendments to the acquisition process ought to be made only after giving wide consideration to the degree's existing international standing. Standing, not in the sense of position on a league table but standing with respect to the acquisition requirements and the fundamental components (lengthy study, original research, thesis preparation). Failing to do so could result in universal reciprocity being lost, as programmes evolving in isolation or without respect to international traditions may subsequently not be considered equivalent. A doctoral programme that does not require a thesis, for example, will most likely not receive the international approval as a doctoral degree may from traditional universities and employers; even though the programme may have exceptional characteristics.

Although this is not yet a problem, reciprocity will no longer exist once aberrant doctoral programmes and/or practices are established. Over the centuries reciprocity has not always been universal (Coulton, 1913: 656, 657) and now that it is, at least between the four countries mentioned, it needs protection. Recently, the Advisory Board for the Research Councils (1993: 2) in Britain has recognized the potentially serious problem of maintaining doctoral standards to protect students and employers.

This monitoring could be carried out through the many professional associations and learned societies that already exist around the world. No special body having monitoring as its primary function ought to be created because competent agencies are already in existence.

7 As has recently been raised, there is a strong need to improve the statistics related to doctoral degree programmes. Cude (1991) writes, '(a)cross the Western world, there is a clear consensus that no definitive statistics exist on the progress of candidates through doctoral programmes'. This failure, to keep these type of statistics and to present them

regularly to the public, could be interpreted as a cover for poor performance at some universities.

Hesseling (1986:98) claims data related to doctoral research and
training is confused because, '(t)here is no sound empirical basis due to the
benign neglect of the past'. Without these doctoral programme statistics,
universities can neither appreciate if problems exist with their programmes, nor plan and implement any innovative solutions to rectify
problems. In addition there can be no international comparison of doctoral
programmes and of those enrolled in them. If the doctoral degree is the
academic laurel so highly prized, it is surprising, and disappointing, we
have so few statistics to describe it and those who would wear it.

Summation

There are many options available when seeking solutions to programme
problems. Some, like defining what is a significant contribution, or
improving adviser–advisee relationships hold merit, but are demanding to
achieve and would necessitate regulations that may be unmanageable.
Solutions such as curtailing the length of the thesis may be highly
appropriate in the humanities, but uncalled for in the physical sciences.
And solutions that reduce the time permitted to complete a doctoral
programme cannot be applied rigidly across the disciplines, or even within
some disciplines because of the nature of certain research.

On the other hand, these seven recommendations are solutions that flow
over all disciplines and they are not drastic departures from existing
practices. In essence these recommendations are:

- Decrease number of entrants into doctoral degree programmes;
- Organize financial independence for non-affiliated students;
- Contract between adviser and advisee to be made mandatory;
- Thesis not to be examined orally (abolish defence/*viva voce*);
- Omit unanimity requirement of the doctoral thesis assessment;
- Reciprocity of all doctoral degree programmes to be protected;
- Statistics of doctoral student progression to be made public.

Of the seven, the most significant would be ensuring full funding for
doctoral students. As soon as the direct expense of limited money becomes
part of a programme, numerous aspects of doctoral programmes, which
hitherto may have received little attention, become important (e.g.
completion rates, research/teaching performance, time to write thesis,
etc.).

As contended, success with improving doctoral degree programmes will
only be had when reforms to the acquisition process are not excessive.
Proposals to initiate major (revolutionary) changes in the programme
format will never be accepted quickly, if at all, even though the new format
may have outstanding attributes. Those who ignore the inertia of the

existing (and historical) acquisition process by quickly implementing major reforms, will most probably see their prized innovations flounder and fail. The author would never recommend that a student enroll in a revolutionary new format doctoral degree programme, on the grounds that academic and institutional inertia would ensure an assessment based on traditional criteria. This would create serious problems for the student.

Proposals to do away with the thesis, or to restrict the absolute time in which a doctoral degree must be achieved, may be doomed in traditional higher education institutions before they are ever implemented. On the latter point Hesseling (1986: 43) points out that the famous French historian Fernand Braudel 'needed more than twenty years to complete his PhD'. Another good example is Albert Einstein, who took six years and two attempts to complete his doctorate.

James (1903) warned us about the doctoral degree over 90 years ago. He wrote, '(w)e ought to look to the future carefully, for it takes generations for a national custom, once rooted, to be grown away from'. Atkinson (1939, 1945: 88) informed us over 50 years ago 'a drastic reform of the PhD is called for'. Surely then the time for change has dawned for us today.

Conclusion

There are a number of actions that could have positive effects on doctoral degrees. Recommendations in this area need to be made with full consideration being given to doctoral degree inertia, that 800-year tendency to maintain the status quo. All institutions are in some way flawed, and the university is no exception. The doctoral degree is not perfect and never will be. To improve it in traditional higher education institutions, small reforms must be implemented, small reforms that nurtured over time can succeed. Not excessive and forced reforms that will be resisted and circumvented. Because, in the language of the original doctorates, *nihil violentum durabit* – nothing that is a source of violence will endure.

Appendix A

First female and male PhD graduates with thesis titles (United States, Canada, Britain, Australia)

United States

1861: Yale University
> Eugene Schuyler: Thesis title is unknown (Schuyler studied botany, metaphysics, modern languages and political science)
> James Morris Whiton: *Ars Longa Brevis Vita*
> Arthur William Wright: *Having Given the Velocity and Direction of Motion of a Meteor Entering the Atmosphere of the Earth, to Determine Its Orbit About the Sun, Taking Into Account the Attractions of Both These Bodies*

1887: Boston University
> Helen Magill: *The Greek Drama*

> *Source:* Xerox University Microfilms (1973: 849, volume 35; 864, volume 37; 991, volume 37; 1064, volume 36)

Canada

1900: University of Toronto
> John Cunningham McLennan: *Electrical Conductivity in Gases Transversed by Cathode Rays*
> William Arthur Parkes: *The Huronian of the Basin of the Moose River*
> Frederick Hughes Scott: *The Structure, Micro-Chemistry and Development of Nerve Cells, With Special Reference to Their Nuclein Compounds*

1903: University of Toronto
> Emma Sophia Baker: *Experiments on the Aesthetic of Light and Colour: On Combination of Two Colours. Spectrally Pure Colours in Binary Combinations*
> Clara Cynthia Benson: *The Rates of Reactions in Solutions Containing Ferrous Sulphate, Potassium Iodide and Chromic Acid*

> *Source:* Mills and Dombra (1968: 24, 60, 109, 125, 131)

Britain

1920: University of Oxford
       James Bronte Gatenby: *The Cyto-Plasmic Inclusions of the Germ Cells*

1922: University of Oxford
       Evelyn Mary Simpson: *The Prose Works of John Donne*

Source: Bailey (1989)

Australia

1948: University of Melbourne
       Claude Charles Joseph Culvenor: *The Chemistry of the Ethylene Sulphides and
           Some Related Topics*
       John Falding McCrea: *Biochemical Aspects of the Virus Haemagglutination
           Phenomenon and the Related Immunological and Serological Problems*
       Rupert Horace Myers: *The Preparation and Properties of Tantalum*
       Joyce Dorothea Stone: *Virus Haemagglutination: A Review of the Literature*
       Erika Charlotte Wolff: *A French-Australian Writer: Paul Wenz*

Source: Arthur (1989)

Appendix B

Doctoral degree components and requirements (1989: Australia, Britain, Canada, United States)

Country/Institution	Time[+] min/max	Research[++] requirements	Thesis[#] options
Australia			
Australian National University	2/4	*	none
University of Adelaide	2/4	original and critical thought, significant contribution	none
University of Melbourne	3/*	independent research, significant contribution	none
University of Sydney	2/8	directed independent research, significant contribution to knowledge	none
University of Tasmania	*/*	substantial original contribution to knowledge, related to disciplines	none
Britain			
Brunel University	3/*	original investigation testing an idea, understand relationship to wider field of knowledge	none

Country/Institution	Time[+] min/max	Research[++] requirements	Thesis[#] options
Edinburgh University	*/5	original, significant contribution, knowledge of field, critical judgement, unified work	none
Heriot-Watt University	2/*	independent contribution to knowledge, evidence of originality	none
University of Cambridge	3/*	*	published work
University of Exeter	2/*	*	none
University of Lancaster	3/*	original contribution to knowledge	none
University of Leeds	3/*	original contribution to understanding of research subject	none
University of Stirling	2/6	original investigation, assess ideas critically, relate to wider field	none
University of Wales	3/*	contribution to learning, systematic study related to body of knowledge	none

Canada

Country/Institution	Time[+] min/max	Research[++] requirements	Thesis[#] options
Carleton University	2/*	original research contributing to knowledge	none
Concordia University	*/4	*	none
Dalhousie University	2/*	original scholarship	none
Memorial University of Newfoundland	2/*	original research	none
Queen's University	*/7	original, further knowledge	none
University of Alberta	2/*	meet standards of reputable scholarly publications	none
University of British Columbia	*/6	original research	none
University of Manitoba	*/7	original research or creative scholarship	none
University of New Brunswick	3/*	independent research, significant contribution to knowledge	none

Country/Institution	Time[+] min/max	Research[++] requirements	Thesis[#] options
University of Saskatchewan	*/6	original investigation, mature scholarship, critical judgement, contribution to knowledge	none
University of Toronto	2/6	independent investigation, significant contribution	none
University of Western Ontario	3/*	original contribution	none

United States

California Institute of Technology	3/*	*	journal articles
Colorado State University	*/10	independent intellectual achievement, contribution to wisdom, knowledge or culture of field	none
Columbia University	*/7	original research	none
Cornell University	3/*	imaginative contribution to knowledge	journal articles
Indiana University at Bloomington	*/7	original scholarly contribution, demonstrate critical ability, imagination, and synthesis	none
Johns Hopkins University	*/*	original investigation worthy of publication	none
Massachusetts Institute of Technology	*/*	original research	none
New York University	*/10	scholarly and exhaustive investigation, add to knowledge, or new significant interpretation	none
North Carolina State University	*/10	original investigation, contribution to knowledge	none
Northwestern University	*/10	original and significant research	none
Ohio State University	*/5	scholarly contribution to knowledge	none

Country/Institution	Time[+] min/max	Research[++] requirements	Thesis[#] options
Princeton University	4/*	independent technical mastery, enlarge/modify what is known or new significant treatment	none
Purdue University	*/*	individual research contributing to knowledge	none
Rockefeller University	3/*	significant experimental or theoretical research	none
Rutgers University	3/*	original investigation of problem(s)	none
Stanford University	*/*	original contribution to scholarship or scientific knowledge	none
State University of New York at Stony Brook	*/7	original and significant scholarly investigation	none
Texas A&M University	*/10	independent, original work of creditable literary scholarship	none
University of California at Los Angeles	2/*	independent investigation	none
University of California at San Diego	*/7	*	none
University of Colorado at Boulder	*/6	original investigation, mature scholarship, critical judgement	none
University of Connecticut	2/*	significant contribution to the field	none
University of Florida	*/5	independent investigation	creative writing
University of Georgia	*/6	originality in research, independent scholarship	none
University of Illinois at Chicago	*/9	independent research	none
University of Maryland at College Park	*/4	*	published works
University of Minnesota Twin Cities	*/5	originality, independent investigation contribution to knowledge	published works

Country/Institution	Time[+] min/max	Research[++] requirements	Thesis[#] options
University of New Mexico	*/5	independent research, competency in scholarly exposition	none
University of North Carolina at Chapel Hill	*/8	contribute fresh outlook or knowledge, mastery of methodology	none
University of Rochester	*/7	original, critical or synthetic treatment, independent research	none
University of Southern California	*/8	original investigation, technical mastery, independent research, scholarly ability	none
University of Utah	3/*	original and independent scientific or scholarly research or artistic creativity	none
University of Virginia	3/7	independent research	none
University of Washington	3/*	significant contribution to knowledge, indicates training in research	none
Washington University	3/*	original scholarly work, mastery of knowledge	none

+ time in years
++ university requirements for a doctoral thesis
# options acceptable in lieu of a thesis in some departments and/or under special circumstances
* specific data not readily available

Source: Noble (1992: 140–4)

Appendix C

Works discussing gender discrimination

Anderson, M. (1992) *Imposters in the Temple: American Intellectuals are Destroying our Universities and Cheating our Students of their Future*. London: Simon and Schuster.

Caplan, P. J. (1992) *Lifting a Ton of Feathers: A Woman's Guide to Surviving in the Academic World*. Toronto: University of Toronto Press.

Dagg, A. I. and Thompson, P. J. (1988) *MisEducation: Women and Canadian Universities*. Toronto: Ontario Institute for Studies in Education.

Dziech, B. W. and Weiner, L. (1991) *The Lecherous Professor*. Baltimore: University of Illinois Press.

Heinrich, K. T. (1991) 'Loving partnerships: dealing with sexual attraction and power in doctoral advisement relationships'. *Journal of Higher Education*, 62(5): 514–38.

Lie, S. S. and O'Leary, V. E. (eds) (1990) *Storming the Tower: Women in the Academic World*. London: Kogan Page.

McLean, T. (1981) *The Black Female PhD*. Washington: University Press of America.

Moore, R. (1985) *Winning the PhD Game*. New York: Dodd Mead.

Moses, I. (1990) *Barriers to Women's Participation as Postgraduate Students*. Canberra: Australian Government Publishing Service.

Paludi, M. A. (1990) *Ivory Power: Sexual Harassment on Campus*. New York: State University of New York Press.

Phillips, E. M. and Pugh, D. S. (1987) *How to Get a PhD*. Milton Keynes: Open University Press.

Powles, M. (1986) 'Chips in the wall? Women and postgraduate study'. *Australian Universities' Review*, 29: 33–7.

Pybus, C. (1993) *Gross Moral Turpitude*. Melbourne: William Heinemann.

Sternberg, D. J. (1981) *How to Complete and Survive a Doctoral Dissertation*. New York: St. Martin's Press.

Sykes, C. J. (1988) *ProfScam: Professors and the Demise of Higher Education*. Washington: Regenery Gateway.

Taylorson, D. (1984) 'The professional socialization, integration and identity of women PhD candidates'. In Acker, S. and Piper, D. W. (eds) *Is Higher Education Fair to Women?* Guildford: Society for Research in Higher Education, NREF-Nelson. 143–62.

Thompson, I. and Roberts, A. (1985) *The Road Retaken: Women Re-enter the Academy.* New York: Modern Language Association of America.

Vartuli, S. (ed) (1982) *The PhD Experience: A Woman's Point of View.* New York: Praeger. 1982.

Williams, E. A., Lam, J. A. and Shively, M. (1992) 'The impact of a university policy on the sexual harassment of females'. *Journal of Higher Education.* 63(1): 50–64.

Appendix D

Scholars who participated in international PhD study (positions and titles at time of survey)

Australia

David Boud, PhD, President, Higher Education Research and Development Society of Australasia

R. G. Hewitt, PhD, Associate Professor: Dean, Faculty of Science, University of Sydney

Thomas Jagtenberg, PhD, Director of Postgraduate Studies, Department of Sociology, University of Wollongong

Bruce, D. Keepes, PhD, Programme Coordinator, College of Advanced Education, Sydney; written on postgraduate supervision

Peggy Nightingale, PhD, Member, Professional Development Centre, University of New South Wales; Editor, Higher Education and Research Development Society of Australasia Bulletin

Britain

Sir Herman Bondi, President, Society for Research into Higher Education; Master of Churchill College, University of Cambridge

David Bottomley, PhD, Assistant Registrar, Council for National Academic Awards

Sir Charles Carter, Member, Policy Studies Institute; former Vice-Chancellor; author of *Higher Education for the Future* (1980)

A. D. Edwards, PhD, Professor; Dean, Faculty of Engineering, Heriot-Watt University

Brian Holmes, PhD, Professor, Institute of Education, University of London; studied and written on higher education degrees

Cari P. J. Loder, Researcher, Centre for Higher Education Studies, Institute of

Education, University of London; PhD degree student; co-author of *Finding Facts Fast* (1991)

Estelle M. Phillips, PhD, Lecturer in Occupational Psychology, Birkbeck College, University of London; involved with the planning of a European doctoral programme; co-author of *How to Get a PhD* (1987)

T. F. Slater, PhD, Professor and Head, Department of Biology and Biochemistry, Brunel University

C. P. Walker, PhD, Head, Criminal Justice Studies, University of Leeds

Canada

Charles H. Bélanger, PhD, Vice-President (Academic), Laurentian University; former Editor, Canadian Journal of Higher Education

Sheryl Bond, PhD, Director, Centre for Higher Education Research, University of Manitoba

Helen J. Breslauer, PhD, Senior Research Officer, Ontario Confederation of University Faculty Associations

Ingrid Bryan, PhD, Dean, Faculty of Arts, Ryerson Polytechnic Institute

Ronald J. Duhamel, PhD, Former Professor, University of Manitoba; co-author of *Academic Futures* (1987); Member of National Parliament

Naomi L. Hersom, PhD, President, Mount St Vincent University; President, Canadian Society for the Study of Higher Education

Kenneth R. Hughes, PhD, President, Canadian Association of Graduate Schools; Dean of Graduate Studies, University of Manitoba

Christopher Ross, PhD, Associate Professor, Graduate Studies and Research, Concordia University; Director, Joint PhD Management Programme

Barry D. McLennan, PhD, Associate Dean, College of Graduate Studies and Research, University of Saskatchewan

Emile Skamene, PhD, Senior Immunology Physician, Montreal General Hospital; Associate Professor, McGill University

David Thompson, PhD, Senior Immunology Physician, Montreal General Hospital; Associate Professor, McGill University

Norman E. Wagner, PhD, Chairman of the Board, Alberta Natural Gas Company Limited; member, Canadian Society for the Study of Higher Education

Cicely Watson, PhD, Professor and Higher Education Chairperson, Ontario Institute for Studies in Education

United States

Arden Albee, PhD, Graduate Studies Dean, California Institute of Technology* (offers PhD thesis option)

Jerold W. Apps, PhD, Professor, Continuing Education, University of Wisconsin (Madison)*; author of *Higher Education in a Learning Society* (1988)

Adrianna Arzac, PhD, Executive Director, International Society for Intercultural Education, Training and Research

Eula Bingham, PhD, Dean, Graduate Studies and Research, University of Cincinnati*

Robert M. Bock, PhD, Dean, Graduate School, University of Wisconsin (Madison)*

William F. Brazziel, PhD, Coordinator, Higher Education Programmes, University of Connecticut*; written on corporate PhD programmes

Lyle D. Calvin, PhD, Dean, Graduate School, Oregon State University*

Walter O. Carlson, PhD, Associate Vice-President, Research and Graduate Studies, Georgia Institute of Technology*

D. Stanley Carpenter, PhD, Executive Secretary-Treasurer, Association for the Study of Higher Education

Allison P. Casarett, PhD, Dean, Graduate School, Cornell University* (offers PhD thesis option)

John W. Chandler, PhD, President, Association of American Colleges

John H. D'Arms, PhD, President, Association of Graduate Schools of the Association of American Universities

Gale Dick, PhD, Dean, Graduate School, University of Utah*

John Dowling, PhD, Distinguished Professor of Romance Languages; former Dean, Graduate School, University of Georgia*

Russell Edgerton, PhD, President, American Association for Higher Education

Stephen Fienberg, PhD, Dean, College of Humanities and Social Sciences, Carnegie-Mellon University*

Bruce Francis, PhD, Vice-President of Academic Affairs, Walden University (adults only university)

Maria Emma Garcia, PhD, 1987 PhD thesis – *Preventing the 'All But Thesis' Phenomenon*; Associate, Ronningen Research and Development Company

Claire Gaudiani, PhD, Project Director, Academic Alliances

Russell G. Hamilton, PhD, Dean, Vanderbilt University*; Board member, Council of Graduate Schools and Association of Graduate Schools

Jerry S. Herron, PhD, Assistant Professor, Wayne State University; author of *Universities and the Myth of Cultural Decline* (1988)

Robert T. Holt, PhD, Dean, Graduate School, University of Minnesota (Twin Cities)*

Charles L. Hostler, PhD, Vice-President Research, Graduate School, Pennsylvania State University*

John J. Koran, PhD, Associate Dean, Graduate School, University of Florida* (offers PhD thesis option)

Jules B. LaPidus, PhD, President, Council of Graduate Schools

Judith S. Liebman, PhD, Dean, Graduate College, University of Illinois (Urbana-Champaign)*

C. W. Minkel, PhD, Dean, Graduate School, University of Tennessee (Knoxville)*

Thomas H. Moss, PhD, Dean, Graduate Studies and Research, Case Western Reserve University*

Thomas B. Peters, PhD, Director, Graduate Records, University of Connecticut*; recent doctoral graduate (1989), thesis topic on doctoral programme review

Allen Plotkin, PhD, Chairman, Aerospace Department Chairmen's Association

W. Werner Prange, PhD, Former Vice-Chancellor, University of Wisconsin (Green Bay); co-author of *Tomorrow's Universities* (1982)

W. C. Royster, PhD, Vice-President, Research and Graduate Studies, University of Kentucky*

Jack H. Schuster, PhD, Associate Professor of Education and Public Policy, and Director of PhD programme in higher education, Claremont Graduate School; co-author of *American Professors: A National Resource Imperiled* (1986)

Judson, D. Sheridan, PhD, Dean, Graduate School, University of Missouri (Columbia)*

Roger H. Sublett, PhD, Executive Vice-President, Association for Continuing Higher Education

Arthur C. Washington, PhD, Executive Secretary, National Institute of Science

James P. White, PhD, Legal Education Consultant, Association of American Law Schools

Edward N. Wilson, PhD, Dean, Graduate School of Arts and Sciences, Washington University*

Gene L. Woodruff, PhD, Dean, Graduate School, University of Washington*

Edwin Yamauchi, PhD, Director, Institute for Biblical Research, Miami University

	females	*males*	
Composition: Australia	1	4	5
Britain	2	7	9
Canada	5	8	13
United States	7	33	40
Totals:	**15**	**52**	**67**

* Leading institution in United States for granting doctoral degrees and conducting research (*Chronicle of Higher Education*, 1988: 64)

Source: Noble (1992: 160–4)

Appendix E

PhD Problems described in international PhD study* (1989: Australia, Britain, Canada, United States)

Australia

1. The number of courses prior to beginning the thesis.
2. Whether there should be a PhD, or similar degree, which is entirely by course work.
3. Whether it is possible to complete part or all of the degree by correspondence study.

4. The degree to which the thesis attempts to investigate a significant issue, as opposed to an issue which is do-able in the time available.
5. The degree to which the student is involved in a team effort, i.e., cooperative research.
6. The scope of the different types of theses which are acceptable.

7. The amount of supervision offered at each stage in the development of the thesis.
8. The degree of specificity, completeness, of the thesis proposal.
9. The minimum and maximum time allowed for the thesis to be completed.

10. There is no prescribed study for most PhD candidates in Australian universities. Where coursework has been proposed as a required element, it has been attacked as lowering the standard of the degree, which is a *research* degree.

* The verbatim response of each scholar is separated by a space. The problems as they relate to the three fundamental components, lengthy study, original research and thesis preparation in that order, are grouped and separated by a half space. Although asked to list three problems for each of the three fundamental components, some scholars listed less, some more and some none. To ensure anonymity, the order of the issues listed here does not correspond with the alphabetical order of the scholars.

11. Many students would benefit from structured and coherent instruction in research methods, but such instruction is almost never offered, much less required.
12. Students attempting PhDs in areas of study which do not have a research tradition (law, computer science) or in interdisciplinary areas (women's studies, aboriginal studies) should not be expected to earn a degree by research only. They need the support and interaction coursework can provide.
13. There is a serious conflict between the two major views of the PhD: (a) that it provides training in research with a view to producing an independent researcher; (b) that the student must make a substantial and original contribution to knowledge.
14. Supervisors and students fail to define sensible and manageable projects which can be completed within minimum enrolment periods.
15. Supervisors all too often allow students to drift along without producing results at regular intervals, and then wonder why students don't complete theses on time (or at all).
16. Standards by which theses are to be judged are incredibly vague. Criteria for evaluation are virtually nonexistent.
17. Theses extending to more than one volume, or well over 500 pages, are all too common.
18. Too little emphasis is placed on editing the thesis to produce coherent and well-structured scholarly writing.

19. Amount of study necessary before starting thesis or research component; how much independent study is required for a PhD.
20. Tension between study component as an induction into an existing body of knowledge versus opening up new areas.
21. Need for courses which are a suitable pre-requisite to independent study versus fitting into existing masters programs. This is difficult for schools with small numbers of students.

22. Ensuring that completion times/rates are not excessive, i.e. student continues far beyond maximum.
23. Relationships between student and adviser; personal mentoring versus getting a product.
24. Appropriateness of standard form of thesis and the fact that they cannot be published without substantial changes in form.
25. Ensuring that maximum length guidelines are adhered to.
26. Ensuring that theses are *theses*, not just accounts of research completed.

Britain

27. Having to spend time on topics with which they are already familiar, e.g. statistics, methodology.
28. Having to spend time on topics which are perceived as irrelevant to what they want to do.
29. Feeling that nobody is interested in what they are doing. Being isolated from others pursuing research objectives.

30. Difficulties in determining what is required, e.g. what are the definitions of quality? originality?
31. Difficulties in pacing work: organizing, planning, managing research.

32. Actually writing it.
33. Getting the correct balance of theoretical underpinning to pragmatic findings/empirical evidence.
34. Being able to select what to put in it and what to leave out – students usually want to write three or four times more than is necessary because they are unable to reject anything that they have done during the course of their work.

35. Lack of a sufficiently clear profile of each candidate's research training needs, so that prescribed courses (where there are any) tend not to fit the needs of individual candidates.
36. Staff/faculty lacking in understanding of the study needs of candidates, and therefore not providing good courses for them.
37. Considerable differences in the interpretation of PhD requirements, for some subjects there is a clear study component (and an emphasis on cooperative research) while for others the candidate is left to obtain study help on his own initiative.

38. Excessive stress on originality leading to work on subjects of no real interest, just because no one has done them before.
39. Ill-defined relations with the 'real world': Institutions differ greatly in their willingness to accept research experience gained in the course of employment.
40. Too much stress on what will (supposedly) please the examiner, as against making a contribution to a wider scholarly or practical community.

41. Tendency to write, at excessive length, in a pretentious jargon. Insufficient stress on communicating ideas in an economic and effective way.
42. Lack of guidance about time required for thesis writing, leading to great delays in final submission.
43. Inadequate skills in presenting background material effectively, without giving an excessive number of useless references (to show how clever you are!).

44. The component is usually too small and minor in UK universities.
45. The relevance of the courses to the work of the student must exist and must be sold to him.
46. The component gives an opportunity for brilliant lectures that is only rarely used to the full.

47. Choice of too difficult a topic makes students take too long (3 years should be the maximum).
48. Topic may be controversial but should be of interest to others in the field.

49. An excellent opportunity to improve the student's ability to communicate. Too rarely used for this purpose.
50. Student not aware of how long good writing takes, nor how demanding a task it is.
51. Student not sufficiently prepared to write well.

52. The identification of 'the problem' to be investigated. This requires that the technical problem to be studied is operationalised in a way which can be repeated by subsequent researchers. How do problems arise? Dewey would say as a result of a sudden unexpected change. This enables the problem to be operationalised.

53. To adopt and thoroughly understand the research methodology appropriate to an investigation of the problem. There are several from which to choose, it is necessary for students to have a good theoretical knowledge of the *appropriate* research technique.

54. Formulation of hypotheses to be tested. These can be regarded as tentative solutions to the problem to be studied. Whether the intention is to confirm or refute the proposed solution will depend on the epistemological assumptions accepted.

55. The purpose of the research depends on whether it is regarded as 'applied' or 'pure' research. If the former, the intention should be to assess the appropriateness of an accepted solution to the conditions under which it is to be applied. The purpose of 'pure' research is to discriminate between hypothetical solutions with the intention of eliminating those which will not work. In other words the purpose can be an overtly 'practical' or 'theoretical' understanding.

56. According to the purpose of the study and the epistemology adopted, the refutation of proposed solutions or the confirmation of stated hypotheses. This problematic bears on the audience, e.g. business, public authorities, etc., to whom the research is addressed. Few public bodies want researchers to demonstrate that their policies will not work. Consequently, if the research is designed to help (or is financed by) industry/public authorities choice of emphasis is important.

57. From my perspective it is imperative to identify the *specific conditions* under which a solution is to be implemented. This is more difficult to realise, other than by using inadequate factorial analysis methods. The identification and weighting of the contextual variables is highly problematic.

Canada

58. The conflict between courses that provide information about administration [generic sense] and courses that are specialised in nature. Our PhD degree is a degree in administration but students belong to departments.

59. Lack of general agreement among professors as to what constitutes core knowledge either in administration generally or in the specialised disciplines.

60. Unwillingness of professors to work with students, or to mount PhD-level courses because of lack of perceived rewards.

61. Different perceptions among faculty as to what is suitable doctoral research.

62. Conflict between quantitative types and qualitative types. Rigor versus relevance issue.

63. Financial support for doctoral students.

64. Putting together a committee of four professors who may each have different notions of what constitutes a thesis.

65. Dealing with students who may be writing a thesis while being employed elsewhere – they are slow. Supervisors leave and they must start all over again.
66. Applied versus theoretical thesis.

67. The purpose of a PhD may be most problematic, especially for people in a professional field like educational administration. Clarifying its purpose in the minds of students and faculty, is essential.
68. Content of the course work should be tailored to individual's background – gaps in domains of knowledge and experience. Emphasis on understanding ways of thinking should have priority.
69. Opportunities to have one's ideas, and to develop the capacity to use criticism constructively is often best found during seminar-type discussions. Keen fellow students and faculty are needed.
70. Research study and completion through to publication is essential part of PhD program. I would not substitute anything else for it.
71. Many candidates are unable to put their own work into some kind of context when discussing their findings. We in the universities should devise ways of preparing them better to do that.
72. The conceptual framework devised by the researcher or adopted for the purpose of the study, is probably the most important part of the whole undertaking.

73. Whether the thesis becomes a book publication or not, it should be of a standard that it should meet such requirements. The student should expect such an outcome and the program should include an introduction to ways of becoming a published author.
74. A thesis may take different forms of publication – video or computer program, or disc, but it should be in a form that can be explained, justified, defended, and contributes to knowledge.
75. Ability to communicate one's ideas in written form, or some other form which can be shared with others, is essential.

76. Not enough course work on methodology. Recipients become totally dependent on technicians for selection of instruments.
77. Many thesis directors are simply not qualified to direct because they have received no methodology and have no non-academic experience.
78. Can one get a PhD in anything and nothing?

79. In many fields theses are endless stacks of paper which could be summarized in a few pages.
80. In professional areas there should be more practicum associated with the PhD requirements.
81. Too many theses conclude with 'more research is needed'. Doesn't that make one wonder?

82. Too long in many fields.
83. Some faculty are not qualified.
84. Some universities take pride in keeping their PhD students 7–9 years. This is objectionable.
85. A thesis is a large book. It's usually the first one a student has written entirely on his/her own. I find students cannot write with precision for the accurate

transfer of information and ideas. Their language is sloppy and their vocabulary cliché ridden. Quite quickly by tearing apart their first chapter almost line by line and editing it you can make them very language conscious and improve their writing.

86. The number of courses required in experimental [name of subject and university deleted] interferes, especially in the first year, with the students' research.
87. At [name of university deleted] there is a necessity of having 18 course credits in experimental medicine. This seems to be rather rigid.
88. Many of my students are foreign and do not have a good grasp of English. Consequently, they may do poorly in their course work because of their inability to express themselves well. In the laboratory, their ability does not prevent conceptualization or performance.
89. A major problem for any graduate student is finding personal financial support. The amount of loans available for graduate students is inadequate.
90. Students do not seem to know the literature related to their research as well as I would expect during the time of doing their bench work.
91. Learning how to design experiments and use appropriate controls to validate and answer the questions posed.
92. Students often spend 6–7 months in the laboratory writing their thesis. An inordinate amount of time is spent writing their thesis. If theses were limited to not more than 100 pages, mandatory presentations of research on a yearly basis, and a vigorous defense would give similar end results.
93. Many theses are unnecessarily long and incorporate a great deal of irrelevant data. Introductions are especially long.
94. Students need practice writing. A better option might be yearly short written reports of 15–20 pages and presentations to department and outside department members.

95. Students apply to the PhD and EdD programs with a variety of MAs not necessarily in education. The university persists in regarding them as having 'transferred field' and requires about four extra preliminary courses – even though their interest and their MA is excellent and adequate background.
96. The PhD requires two *consecutive* academic years of residence [full-time study], the EdD one. It should be possible to start the PhD course work part time (as in the EdD) and to break up the residence years allowing for return to work. Most doctoral candidates these days are not 22-year-old youngsters.
97. Both doctorates' full-time work permission is predicted on a university-type academic workload, unrealistic for candidates who have other jobs, and that's increasingly common. It's defined as maximum ten hours. It could be ten hours of teaching and permissible! A student could be the mother of ten school-aged children and be considered unemployed.
98. Difficulty of access to [illegible word here] and subjects. My students often wish to study the university itself [illegible word here] institutions, look at their records and policies. For institutions committed to *doing* research, the members are strangely cosy.
99. Cost. Too many theses are carried out with very small [illegible word here] because of time and dollar costs. Postage, telephone, travel, printing of flyers,

etc., commuting runs to over $2,000–$3,000. Not all students have SSHRC grants. The research is adequate but has to be characterized as an 'introductory pilot' or 'case study'.

100. I think research *originality* must be stressed. I do not agree with theses which merely synthesize known literature. I think *time* is essential. I assume research training will be adequate and required. What is needed is *honest* counselling of candidates so they know the whole program will probably take five years beyond masters.

101. The problem of getting students to define a researchable question *before* approval is given for them to begin work is not generally faced by faculty. Too often the weaknesses emerge after the thesis work has begun.

102. Faculty, for the most part, have never been taught to direct someone else's research. They are too 'approving', don't offer enough direction. They are vague and general in their responses instead of being *specific* and *prescriptive*.

103. Faculty are lazy – too slow in their response time and apt to wait for the student to come with a problem instead of periodically *requiring* face-to-face progress reports.

104. Availability of courses – some courses are offered in alternate years or at a time which conflicts with another course.

105. Relevance of course work to the proposed research. Sometimes courses do not seem to be of any use to the proposed research.

106. Credit for courses taken by independent study or distance education. To give credit for such work how do you assess the quality and ensure the student has access to library resources?

107. Lack of financial support for research constrains the amount and kind of research which can be done.

108. Relevance of the proposed research or benefit to the community outside the academic environment. Particularly true for international students.

109. Availability of financial assistance for the student – some students cannot afford to go to a doctoral program because of lack of personal finances.

110. Quality of thesis supervision. How does a student select a good supervisor?

111. Variation in expectations and standards between departments or institutions.

112. Options in lieu of a thesis – published papers and/or a thesis. Suitable for some disciplines but not all. How do you know who did the work?

113. The difficulty of having courses from other disciplines recognized as part of the course of study.

114. Lack of opportunity to take courses part time.

115. Lack of good teaching.

116. Difficulties in doing interdisciplinary research.

117. Financial support.

118. Lack of advice or supervision.

119. Inadequate supervision.

120. In general I was satisfied with my experience as a doctoral student. I had some difficulties in getting my supervisor to read completed chapters within a reasonable time period.

121. Length of time taken to complete requirements.
122. Required courses – fitting them in, integrating them with others, leaving enough time for individually tailored courses.
123. Formal vs. informal opportunities for study – the importance of learning from peers and interacting informally in a graduate student subculture.

124. Balancing interest in the subject matter with relevance to both the discipline and life itself.
125. Limiting the scope of the topic, i.e. making a realistic assessment of what can be done in the course of one research project.
126. Getting good advice and guidance from a supervisor, both with respect to [respondent refers to the issues numbered 124 and 125] and on a contextual basis as the research develops.

127. The amount of time taken to finish it – it should not be allowed to become a life's work. Although difficult to grasp at the time, this needs to be kept in perspective. Flexibility, however, for those engaged in other activities while writing, e.g. working, bearing or raising children.
128. The length of the thesis – for much the same reason as [scholar refers to issue number 127]. Good advising here could assist in keeping his under control.
129. Departmental and university rules should not be allowed which turn back a thesis for anything other than minor changes. Students should not be allowed to proceed to the point of starting a thesis or be allowed to engage in all the research and writing involved and then be turned back. The thesis defense should not be an opportunity to 'weed out' students.

130. Length of time required to complete the study portion. PhD program has been and will continue to be problematic. Amount of study is directly related to this time. Full-time study can be especially difficult. What is needed is a 'defined number of courses' – when necessary – and flexibility in time arrangements – length and when done.
131. The method of study – formal classroom setting versus readings or . . . needs to be explained. Each method is valid. Approach may be related primarily to the focus of the doctorate, its nature, the students' preferences and so on.
132. What is an appropriate background for study at the doctoral level? What constitutes an appropriate doctoral thesis? These questions must be explored and the responses need to be more clearly articulated than they are – at least in most instances.

133. Is the purpose of the research clear – in terms of the student's further needs in his/her doctoral program? Is the research intended primarily for the student's academic and professional growth?
134. Will the research emphasize the student's academic and/or professional needs? Must the research be supervised by one or more individuals?
135. What is appropriate research in terms of the student's eventual goal – which could be to successfully complete a PhD which will improve his skills knowledge level.
136. The scope of a thesis – because its breadth often varies from one adviser to the next needs to be better understood. How much 'depth' must it contain?
137. The intent should be originality and/or new insights/knowledge – when possible. Confirmation may be sufficient in certain cases.

138. There should be options in lieu of a thesis – supervised practicum. Publication of a book should be an accepted substitute – with certain conditions.

United States

139. Curriculum design: The curriculum quite often seems to be determined by the personal interest of the faculty in the department, rather than the evaluation of skills that need to be acquired for professional success. Results: take unnecessary courses.
140. Lack or insufficient practica: A higher percentage of courses in the doctoral program seem to be theoretical, rather than applications of knowledge to real settings.
141. Requirements like competency exams and review papers are often quite [illegible word here]. Neither the faculty nor the students know what to do about it.
142. Define a research topic. Most faculty have difficulty coming up with a worthwhile research topic, and they expect inexperienced researchers to be able to define a better research than they themselves could do.
143. Make an original contribution. This tradition of research as a 'new [illegible word here] in the ever growing temple of knowledge' doesn't help much. Research project should attempt to solve practical problems, this might involve replication studies.
144. Human subjects or animal subjects rights committees. Today the research are stopped or delayed for unreasonable requests from human and animal subjects rights committees. They sometimes seem to have lost sight of what research are all about.
145. Supervision by faculty: Supervisors give too much freedom to the students, because it takes too much time for them to supervise research.
146. Write the final thesis. A difficult task that requires many rewritings. Because of usual lack of supervision, this becomes a serious problem at the time of writing the doctoral thesis.
147. Disagreement over thesis requirements between faculty. Departmental faculty should define what is a good thesis and agree on thesis requirements. Quite often, the student's thesis becomes the excuse for methodological and technical arguments between faculty. This often results in increasing time to graduation.

148. Insufficient interdisciplinary emphasis.
149. Although not always applicable, PhD study programs generally take too little account of the needs of those who will pursue teaching careers, especially those who will be teaching undergraduate students.
150. Insufficient attention to the history and methodology of the discipline.

151. Too much stress on individual research, too little provision for team research, especially in humanities and social sciences.
152. Too little use of foreign languages as research tools.
153. Topic too often too narrow because of stress upon making original contribution to scholarship.
154. Stress upon single product. Why not a series of essays, experiments?

155. Too much stress upon originality, too little attention to the training and educational value of doing thesis.

156. Relevant courses – very often doctoral students are advised to take courses that have little or no significance in impacting their present or future endeavors. Course work should be selected and developed with the intent of helping students understand research and the importance of qualitative and quantitative thinking.

157. Number of courses – the number of courses or semester/quarter credits that one takes toward partially fulfilling requirements for the PhD should vary according to the determined academic preparation of students. Nevertheless, it must be remembered that the PhD is a research-focused degree and not designed for an abundance of course work.

158. Seminars – some structured course work (i.e. regular classroom teaching) is necessary. However, seminars are very important in developing qualitative thinking skills of students. Increasingly, participatory seminars (student presentations) should be incorporated in the PhD program.

159. Purpose of research – the original intent of performing research for the PhD degree was to sharpen the mind, develop students with sophisticated, highly trained, and heightened intellectual skills. The focus continues today. However, the search for specific answers to problems has led to the development of dishonesty in researchers. The end point of research for the PhD in science, engineering, and mathematics is too narrowly focused.

160. Emphasis of research – it is my opinion that too little emphasis is placed on research. The PhD degree has moved more toward course requirements.

161. Financial assistance – in most cases doctoral students are not adequately compensated for the jobs done for the various universities and colleges. Doctoral students serve as teaching assistants or research assistants. They are employed on a half-time basis (20 work hours/week). This time contracted is theoretical and far less time than that required for the job.

162. A full-time residency requirement.

163. An emphasis on the relationship of theory to practice.

164. Acceptance of doctorates within the university community.

165. Basic versus applied research.

166. Funding for research.

167. Nature of research for part-time students.

168. Thesis structure to fit the research rather than a prescribed chapter outline.

169. Publication of a book or monograph in lieu of a thesis.

170. For certain research topics, a writing style for those who can use the results.

171. Courses may repeat material which has been covered in previous work (at other universities or in the same one).

172. There is rarely a true attempt to integrate courses. This results in a 'string of pearls' program.

173. Many courses are taught in a traditional mode, not allowing the student to use creativity and/or thinking skills.

174. Not enough research other than the thesis is required. The student winds up doing a dissertation as his/her first piece of research.

175. Research that is done is most often designed by a supervisor. The student is rarely required to be original.
176. Research is often quite narrow in focus, hence unrelated to the overall program.
177. The thesis is usually treated as a solitary activity as opposed to 'real world' research which is usually collaborative.
178. Since this is often the first piece of research completed by the student, an expectation of originality and importance is somewhat unreasonable.
179. There is a ticklish balance between quality and completion. The thesis becomes the 'last hoop' and research suffers.

180. Course requirements – should all doctoral candidates be required to complete certain basic methodological/pedagogical courses as point of departure for later specialized study?
181. Should graduate seminars, especially those purporting to be 'surveys' enabling candidates to gain advanced comprehension of entire subject areas (e.g. literary eras) incorporate the seminar professor's personal 'special topic' preference as its focus? It may contradict the purpose.
182. Should all graduate programs in the same field require a certain number of courses before students proceed to thesis research? (How shall candidates demonstrate readiness for the research?)

183. How shall candidates be held accountable during research phase? Do guidelines need to be enacted for advisers and their students to discuss/ensure validity, thoroughness, originality, significance of research?
184. Where will money come from to support students doing research.

185. Should relations between adviser(s) and thesis writer be more structured. Should more be done about articulating to the writer the form and style peculiar to theses (i.e. stylistic/formal instruction).
186. Is original scholarship a must? Or would it suffice to let the thesis demonstrate competent relations between discrete ideas and collected information?
187. Does a prescribed length only encourage irrelevance and bloated organization?

188. Should graduate students be exposed to formal experiences (courses, seminars, etc.) dealing with ethics and nature of research?
189. Should graduate students be exposed to formal experiences dealing with teaching in their disciplines and in higher education?
190. Should graduate students have to 'minor' in a subject related to their 'major'?

191. Too much emphasis on applied versus basic. Increasing pressure to do developmental projects. Emphasis on short term goals (although not necessarily on short time to degree).
192. Most research by graduate students is on projects obtained by their advisers. Originality of concept is not often encountered.
193. Group or teaching research brings into question the idea of independent investigation.

194. Do dissertations serve as scholarly resources or are they anachronisms?
195. Is the preparation of a dissertation a waste of time in fields where publication is in the form of short articles?

196. Do faculty advisers exert enough influence in *limiting* the scope of the dissertation so that it is realistic?

197. Often, courses are offered at the faculty member's rather than the student's convenience, required courses are offered infrequently, key courses are scheduled in conflict with other heavily subscribed courses, required prerequisites cause sequencing problems, etc.

198. The proper balance in the course work phase between breadth and depth can be difficult to achieve. Certainly, a doctorally prepared scholar should be a specialist, but he/she should also possess substantial knowledge of a general sort in his/her field.

199. Course requirements should not be so onerous that they impede *unreasonably* the student's progress in taking exams, satisfying language or skill requirements, conducting research, and writing the dissertation.

200. There are those studies which seem to be of limited significance. Research should constitute a *useful* contribution to the body of knowledge in the field of study. Studies that follow should be able to build on the findings of the research.

201. The novelty of the research is an important factor. Much research is not on the 'cutting edge'. Many studies deal with familiar topics with only *slight* variations or modifications to distinguish them from earlier studies.

202. Research is expensive. Doctoral students often are of modest means. Institutional and/or external support is helpful but often inadequate.

203. Many doctoral students do not sufficiently define and limit the parameters of the study. As a consequence, coherence and internal organization suffer and the dissertation lacks focus.

204. Many doctoral students have not learned to write cogently and succinctly. Many have the idea that the doctoral dissertation *has to be* lengthy. Simple statements are more effective than convoluted sentences.

205. Many students prolong the process unnecessarily because of an overwhelming concern about perfection. Often, faculty advisers on a student's committee are not in agreement about necessary editorial and organizational changes.

206. Achievement of breadth in the field of the PhD – learning both the field, its development as an academic discipline and the methodologies and critical frameworks for the field.

207. Achievement of knowledge related to the field of the PhD (historians need literature and philosophy as well as political science). Political scientists need history, literature, philosophy, etc.

208. Achievement of knowledge in the pedagogy of the discipline. How is *this* knowledge imparted to different learners, etc.

209. Reading before the dissertation topic designed to develop a grasp of the major issues bearing on the subject.

210. Insistence by research advisers on the significance of the topic to the discipline.

211. Exposure to range of research methods and their relationships to outcomes and the politics of the discipline.

212. A thesis should continue to be a major piece of research notable for its depth and breadth of contribution to the field.

213. Its progress should be the ongoing serious concern of several faculty members who are publishing scholars.
214. Thesis should make a notable contribution to the individual and the discipline.

215. Achieving breadth as well as depth in preparation for thesis *and* for future research.
216. Keep study within reasonable time limit.
217. Poor preparation – too many basics (including languages) covered during graduate work.
218. Available financial support controls area of research.
219. Areas of research too closely tied to adviser's research because of funding situation.
220. Bias to 'large lab group' research in many fields.
221. Limit time of thesis research.
222. Scope of thesis – preparation for a career vs. magnus opus.
223. Acceptance of published material as part of thesis – question of authorship on such papers.

224. Should students in US history be required to have skills in such traditional languages as French and German? Can he/she substitute a discipline such as statistics? How many languages should those in ancient history be required to have? (Greek, Latin, Hebrew, others?)
225. Should doctoral students have an acquaintance with various philosophies of history, e.g. Marxism? How large a component of required courses should be in historiography and/or intellectual history? Should we have other requirements than these oriented about regions and eras?
226. How concentrated or diverse should the candidate's fields be? A major field and a minor field would concentrate the candidate's efforts upon the areas of his dissertation. On the other hand, competency in a broad range of fields (three to four), would make the candidate more marketable, especially for jobs in small colleges.

227. How much of a stipend should be given? What duties should be required? Is it reasonable to ask a teaching fellow to teach two sections of a survey course? How many years support should a student be given? Is three years too short a period of time?
228. Should a student be restricted to materials which are available to him locally? If he has to use interlibrary services, should there be a limit to his use of these? What support should the university give to its graduate programs in terms of its library resources?
229. Should a student be assisted in his travels to visit repositories of documents? What about travel abroad? Should a student be aided to attend a conference, when he reads a paper? What if he/she simply attends?

230. What efforts should be made to ensure that the topic of the thesis falls within the competence of the thesis adviser? If he or she is not fully confident, should an outside adviser be invited to participate. If so, at what kind of compensation?
231 What role should be played by the other readers of the dissertation? Should the student give first drafts to them chapter by chapter, or only drafts revised

in the light of the adviser's comments? Should the other readers' comments be limited to coherence rather than content?

232. What should be the length of time permitted for the completion of a dissertation? Should there be a limit placed on the length of the dissertation? Should the student strive to produce a publishable work?

Source: Noble (1992: 177–92)

Appendix F

Terms associated with doctoral research

Originality

'What is original may not be significant and what is significant may not be original,' remarked one graduate dean in reference to Berelson's now classic discussion of the traditional conception of the dissertation. Thirty years ago Berelson was at pains to point out that the notion of the dissertation as an original and significant contribution to knowledge was only a statement of intent. Definition of the terms was left to the departments, and serious questions were being raised not only about the realization but about the appropriateness of the aim.

The idea of originality was especially suspect given the extent of team research in the sciences, and the notion of 'significant contribution to knowledge' received some hard questioning as well. According to Berelson's findings, the alternative to judging the dissertation by these traditional terms was to consider it an instrument of research training, 'a trial run in scholarship and not a monumental achievement. The primary test would be, in other words, whether it contributed to the student's knowledge, not the world's.' When asked, 'should the doctoral dissertation be regarded more as a training instrument than as an original contribution to knowledge?' 55 per cent of the deans, 45 per cent of the graduate faculty, and 40 per cent of the recent degree recipients Berelson surveyed answered yes.

Despite the trend 30 years ago towards judging the dissertation by a different, more realistic standard, originality, significance, and independence have not disappeared from the vocabulary used to describe distinguishing characteristics of the doctoral research project and product. Now, as then, defining the terms is difficult, and they continue to mean different things in different fields.

Citing Supreme Court Justice Potter Stewart's frustrated statement that he could not define pornography but that he knew it when he saw it, one university report suggested that defining originality presented similar difficulties. In its most general sense, 'original' describes research that has not been done previously or a project that creates new knowledge; it implies that there is some novel twist, fresh perspective, new hypothesis, or innovative method that makes the dissertation project a distinctive contribution. An original project, although built on existing research, should not duplicate someone else's work.

Significant

Significant as applied to doctoral research projects and dissertations is also subject to debate. A significant piece of work provides information that is useful to other scholars in the field and, ideally, is of such importance that it alters the thinking of scholars in the students' field of study. A further question is whether the dissertation itself is a significant document or whether the term refers only to the nature and quality of the research.

It is difficult, asserts one university report, to argue that dissertations are themselves significant when in many fields they play a minor role as scholarly resources. Particularly in the humanities and the softer social sciences, dissertations are not expected to be cited by scholars in their published work. The notion that doctoral dissertations are significant contributions to knowledge thus seems to represent an ideal rather than a quantifiable fact.

Independence

Independence or autonomy is intertwined with 'originality', and its definition also varies by field. It is dependent on the nature of the research, the resources needed, the adviser's style, practices common to the discipline, and custom in the student's program. According to the report from one university, the experience of most students seems to fall in a three-point spectrum from high to low autonomy.

In the humanities, at the most autonomous end of the spectrum, originality is related closely to independence. A student, although receiving guidance from a dissertation adviser, is usually responsible for both conception and execution of the doctoral research project. Moreover, a teaching assistant's duties, for which the student receives support, are usually unrelated to the dissertation research.

Midway on the independence–autonomy spectrum, a student may develop the idea for the dissertation through interaction with the dissertation director and occasionally with the other committee members, and the dissertation director may apply for a grant to support the research. The faculty adviser may retain full supervisory control of the student's work on the research project or permit the student to proceed independently, merely monitoring the progress of research. Assistantship support is typically provided by the grant.

Autonomy is most constrained in the sciences, where students often join ongoing research projects for which the principal investigator has received funding . . . the idea for the dissertation originates with the principal investigator and grows out of the larger project. The student, whose assistantship is funded by the research grant, must develop, refine, define, and do the research on the topic, contributing to the design of the project, to the measurement and collection of new information, and to the analysis and interpretation of information.

At the low end of the scale when a doctoral student is part of a team pursuing an ongoing research project, the status of the student as an independent researcher is subject to real question and is heavily dependent on the research practices and personality of the principal investigator. In such cases, one university report recommended candid discussion among the faculty, representative students, and the graduate dean, with the objective of encouraging research practices that protect the academic freedom of the faculty and promote the intellectual growth of the individual student.

Despite differences among disciplines, the consensus was that 'original' does not mean 'in isolation'. The idea for the dissertation project and the approach taken need not be developed solely by the student. It is expected, however, that the student should develop and carry out the research project relatively independently and be able to demonstrate to the satisfaction of the advisory committee what portion of the research represents the student's own thinking.

Source: Council of Graduate Schools (1991: 8–10)

Appendix G

Adviser–Advisee contract

We, _____ and _____
        (Adviser)   (Advisee)

willingly enter into a contract with respect to the doctoral degree: _____

in _____.
                        (Field of Specialization)

As the Adviser I, _____ have been informed
by the Advisee of her/his academic background, her/his doctoral research interests,
and of her/his doctoral degree programme intentions.

As the Advisee I, _____ have been informed

by the Adviser that _____ per cent of students enrolling in the above
described doctoral degree programme at the institution named below do not
complete the doctorate, and that the mean time to graduate after enrolling in the

programme is _____ years.

As two people filling historical and honourable roles in academe,

we, _____ and _____
        (Adviser)   (Advisee)

will not exploit each other in any manner, and we will each maintain written records

of all our _____

meetings related to the doctoral degree, and every problem shall, by either party, be brought in writing to the personal attention of,

_____ and _____
(Dean/Director)   (Dept./Division Head)

who as representatives of the Institution shall take immediate steps to rectify the problem and prevent its reoccurrence.

Signed: _____   _____
(Adviser)   (Advisee)

Witness: _____   _____
(Dean/Director)   (Dept./Division Head)

At: _____
(Name of Institution)

City: _____ Date: _____

Addendum

This Adviser–Advisee contract is a sample of what such a document could look like. Two significant questions have been raised by reviewers of the document.

Acknowledging as a given fact that some form of wording could be devised that would meet all expressed important concerns, is such a document necessary? And would advisers and advisees sign such a contract?

Written contracts are entered into when there is a goods and/or services agreement between a minimum of two parties, to ensure that these goods and/or services are transferred, and are transferred in a manner that the parties have previously agreed to. Written contracts usually confirm verbal or tacit agreements, they permit conditions to be clarified to all parties' satisfaction, they protect the interests of the signing parties, and most importantly, they permit and facilitate action that will ensure transferral or compensate for the lack of transferral as agreed to.

Verbal contracts between advisers and advisees already exist in relation to doctoral education. By putting the agreement on paper the process simply becomes more structured, and most importantly, both parties have a constant reminder of their obligations. Here the emphasis is on the word both, because either party (see Ferber, 1960) can suffer from the action or inaction of the other party.

With two witnesses to the contract, who must be informed of any difficulties that occur within the relationship, neither party can continue with unsatisfactory behaviour. Where no written contract exists, the relationship can degenerate to a point where the adviser and/or advisee can suffer greatly because no recourse may be available – without suffering greater loss. Yes, a written contract is necessary.

To the second question raised, one wonders why an adviser and an advisee would not want to sign such a contract. A contract would ensure that both parties have some protection. As both parties are about to invest a good part of their adult life and personal resources into seeing a doctoral programme completed, protecting this investment is a wise move.

Certainly this type of contract protects advisees far more than they are protected now. As it stands, advisees are in the most vulnerable position in doctoral programmes. To speak up about irregularities can mean abandoning all hope of ever attaining a doctorate. Improprieties should not be allowed to continue because an individual is too intimidated to comment.

A contract can confirm to all the signing parties their obligations to the doctoral degree programme as stipulated in the contract. If a contract offers both parties equal protection in the case of litigation, and if it could help them have a better academic and perhaps personal relationship, universities should insist upon an Adviser–Advisee contract.

References

Adams, C. K. (1887) 'University education in the United States'. *Canada Educational Monthly*, April, 131–5; September, 268–73.

Advisory Board for the Research Councils (1993) *Nature of the PhD* (Office of Science and Technology Discussion Document). London: Advisory Board for the Research Councils.

Andersen, D. G. (1983) 'Differentiation of the EdD and PhD in education'. *Journal of Teacher Education*, XXXIV(3), 55–8.

Anderson, M. (1992) *Imposters in the Temple*. New York: Simon and Schuster.

Apps, J. W. (1988) *Higher Education in a Learning Society*. San Francisco: Jossey-Bass.

Archer, E. A. (1992) *Commonwealth Universities Yearbook 1992*. London: Association of Commonwealth Universities.

Arthur A. (1989) Correspondence from Principal Librarian, Baillieau Library, University of Melbourne, 6 September.

Ash, E. *et al.* (1988) *The British PhD*. London: Committee of Vice-Chancellors and Principals of the Universities of the United Kingdom.

Association of American Universities (1990) *Institutional Policies to Improve Doctoral Education*. Washington: Association of American Universities.

Atkinson, C. (1939, 1945) *True Confessions of a PhD and Recommendations for Reform*. Boston: Meador Publishing.

Bailey, S. (1989) Correspondence from Archivist, Bodleian Library, University of Oxford, 18 September.

Becher, T. (1981) 'Towards a definition of disciplinary cultures'. *Studies in Higher Education*, 6(2), 109–22.

Ben-David, J. (1977) *Centers of Learning*. New York: McGraw-Hill.

Bent, H. E. (1959) 'Professionalization of the PhD degree'. *Journal of Higher Education*, XXX(3), 140–5.

Bercuson, D. J., Bothwell, J. and Granatstein, J. L. (1984) *The Great Brain Robbery*. Toronto: McClellan and Stewart.

Berelson, B. (1960) *Graduate Education in the United States*. New York: McGraw-Hill.

Bestor, D. K. (1982) *Aside From Teaching What in the World Can You Do?* Seattle: University of Washington.

Blackett, Lord (1969) *Thoughts on the PhD Degree* (Presidential Address, Anniversary Day). London: Royal Society.

Bladen, V. W. (1962) In Dunton, D. and Patterson, D. (eds) *Canada's Universities in a*

New Age (Conference Proceedings, Canadian Universities and Colleges; November 1961). Ottawa: Le Droit.

Bonneau, L.-P. and Corry, J. A. (1972) *Quest for the Optimum: Research Policy in the Universities of Canada*. Ottawa: Association of Universities and Colleges of Canada.

Bowen, H. R. and Schuster, J. H. (1986) *American Professors: A National Resource Imperiled*. New York: Oxford University Press.

Bowen, W. G. and Rudenstine, N. L. (1992) *In Pursuit of the PhD*. Princeton: Princeton University Press.

Bowen, W. G. and Sosa J. A. (1989) *Prospects for Faculty in the Arts and Sciences*. Princeton: Princeton University Press.

Boyer, E. L. (1988) 'Publish and be damned as a teacher'. *Times Higher Education Supplement*, September 23, 16.

Boyer, E. L. (1990) *Scholarship Reconsidered*. Princeton: The Carnegie Foundation for the Advancement of Teaching.

Braddock, D. (1987) 'The PhD degree'. In Bureau of Labor Statistics (ed.) *Outlook for College Graduates and PhDs*. Washington: Department of Labor.

British Council (1986) *The British PhD and the Overseas Student* (Committee for International Co-operation in Higher Education Report). London: British Council.

Buckley, P. J. and Hooley, G. J. (1988) 'The non-completion of doctoral research in management'. *Educational Research*, 30(2) 110–19.

Canadian Manufacturers' Association (1986) *University Post-Graduate Training* (Science and Technology Committee Report). Ottawa: Canadian Manufacturers' Association.

Carnegie Commission on Higher Education (1971) *Less Time, More Options*. New York: McGraw-Hill.

Carter, C. (1980) *Higher Education for the Future*. Oxford: Basil Blackwell.

Centra, J. A. and Kuykendall, N. M. (1974) *Women, Men and the Doctorate*. Princeton: Educational Testing Service.

Chambers, M. M. (1950) *Universities of the World Outside USA*. Washington: American Council on Education.

Chambers, M. M. (1976) *Keep Higher Education Moving*. Danville: Interstate Printers and Publishers.

Chapman, L. and Webster, F. (1993) 'Measuring quality by the written yard'. *Times Higher Education Supplement*, 26 February, 17.

Christopherson, D. *et al.* (1983) *Research Student and Supervisor*. Swindon: Science and Engineering Research Council.

—— *Chronicle of Higher Education*. (1988) *Almanac*. Washington.

Clarke, S. (1993) Personal communication with Research Degree Officer, Open University, 1 March.

Cobban, A. B. (1975) *The Mediaeval Universities: Their Development and Organization*. New York: Methuen.

Coulton, G. G. (1913) 'Universities'. In Monroe, P. (ed.) *A Cyclopedia of Education*. New York: Macmillan.

Council of Graduate Schools (1977) *The Doctor of Philosophy Degree*. Washington: Council of Graduate Schools.

Council of Graduate Schools (1990a) *Research Student and Supervisor*. Washington: Council of Graduate Schools.

Council of Graduate Schools (1990b) *The Doctor of Philosophy Degree*. Washington: Council of Graduate Schools.

Council of Graduate Schools (1991) *The Role and Nature of the Doctoral Disssertation.* Washington: Council of Graduate Schools.

Courtenay, B. C. (1988) 'Eliminating the confusion over the EdD and PhD in colleges and schools of education'. *Innovative Higher Education,* 13(1), 11–20.

Coyle, S. L. and Thurgood, D. H. (1989) *Summary Report 1987: Doctorate Recipients From United States Universities.* Washington: National Academy Press.

Cross, K. P. (1987) 'The changing role of higher education in the United States'. *Higher Education Research,* 6(2), 99–108.

Crosson, P. H. and Nelson, G. M. (1986) 'A profile of higher education doctoral programs'. *Review of Higher Education,* 9(3), 355–7.

Cude, W. (1987) *The PhD Trap.* West Bay, Nova Scotia: Medicine Label Press.

Cude, W. (1991) 'The need for improved doctoral program statistics'. *Canadian Journal of Higher Education,* XXI(1), 1–6.

Curtis, M. H. (1985) *Integrity in the College Curriculum.* Washington: Association of American Colleges.

D'Arms, J. H. (1990) 'Universities must lead the effort to avert impending national shortages of PhDs'. *Chronicle of Higher Education,* January 17, B1, B3.

Davies, L. W. (1972) 'Federal policies for industries and development in Australia'. *Search,* 3, 423–6.

Davinson, D. (1977) *Theses and Dissertations As Information Sources.* London: Clive Bingley.

Dewey, J. (1917) *Proceedings* (Annual Meeting, Association of American Universities, 9, 10 November, 1917). Washington: Association of American Universities.

Dill, D. D. and Morrison, J. L. (1985) 'EdD and PhD research training in the field of higher education'. *Review of Higher Education,* 8(2), 169–86.

Donald, J. G. (1983) 'Knowledge structures'. *Journal of Higher Education,* 54(1), 31–41.

Draper, H. (1965) *The Mind of Clark Kerr.* New York: Dell Publishing.

Durant, W. (1935) *The Story of Civilization* (Part I): Our Oriental Heritage. New York: Simon and Schuster.

Durant, W. (1939) *The Story of Civilization* (Part II): The Life of Greece. New York: Simon and Schuster.

Durant, W. (1950) *The Story of Civilization* (Part IV): The Age of Faith. New York: Simon and Schuster.

Durant, W. (1957) *The Story of Civilization* (Part VI): The Reformation. New York: Simon and Schuster.

Durant, W. and Durant, A. (1975) *The Story of Civilization* (Part XI): The Age of Napoleon. New York: Simon and Schuster.

Encel, S. (1965) 'The social role of higher education'. In Wheelwright, E. (ed.) *Higher Education in Australia.* Canberra: F. W. Cheshire.

Evangelauf, J. (1989) 'Lengthening of time to earn a doctorate causes a concern'. *Chronicle of Higher Education,* 15 March, A1, A13.

Ferber, R. (1960) 'The administration of the PhD degree'. *Journal of Higher Education,* XXIX(II), 384–91.

Fisher, S. (1987) 'Burning out the best'. *Times Higher Education Supplement,* 3 April, 13.

Frost, S. B. (1967) 'The PhD degree'. *McGill University Bulletin of Educational Procedures,* (Number 11), February.

Garcia, M. E. (1987) *Preventing the 'All But Thesis' Phenomenon* (PhD Dissertation). Kalamazoo: Western Michigan University.

Gerson, M. (1989) 'Shortage of new PhDs is forseen for universities.' *Chronicle of Higher Education*, 3 May, A40.

Gold, K. (1988) 'Researchers need new skills for jobs market'. *Times Higher Education Supplement*, 15 January, 7.

Good, C. V. (1973) *Dictionary of Education*. New York: McGraw-Hill.

Gordy, J. P. (1891) 'Chairs of pedagogy'. *Canada Educational Monthly*, March, 93–8.

Gould, S. B. (ed.) (1974) *Commission on Nontraditional Study*. San Francisco: Jossey-Bass.

Graves, D. (1983) 'Judgements of graduate deans and their reports regarding foreign language requirements for the PhD'. *ADFL Bulletin*, 15(2), 37–9.

Gravesande, D. (1991) *Books in Print 1991–92*. New York: R. R. Bowker.

Green, C. (1977) 'Degrees, diplomas and certificates'. In Knowles, A. S. (ed.) *The International Encyclopedia of Higher Education* (Volume 4). San Francisco: Jossey-Bass.

Grigg, C. M. (1965) 'Types of degrees and graduate programs'. In *Graduate Education*. New York: The Centre for Applied Research in Education.

Grolier Society (1983) *Australian Encyclopedia* (Volume 10). Melbourne: Grolier Society.

Halstead, B. (1987) 'The PhD system'. *Bulletin of the British Psychological Society*, 40, 99–100.

Harmon, L. R. (1978) *A Century of Doctorates: Data Analyses of Growth and Change*. Washington: National Academy of Science.

Harris, R. S. (1976) *A History of Higher Education in Canada 1163–1960*. Toronto: University of Toronto Press.

Helwig, D. (1988) 'The profit-minded professors'. *Canadian Business*, January, 46–9, 82–4.

Heron, E. (1989) 'Cambridge blacklisted in purge on PhD completers'. *Times Higher Education Supplement*, 3 February, 1.

Hesseling, P. (1986) *Frontiers of Learning: The PhD Octopus*. Dordrecht: Foris Publications.

Hill, S. C., Fensham, P. J. and Howden, I. B. (1974) *PhD Education in Australia*. Canberra: Australian Academy of Science.

Hill, S. C. and Johnston, R. (1984) 'Postgraduate education towards the year 2000'. *Higher Education Research and Development*, 3(2), 121–35.

Hockey, J. (1991) 'The social science PhD: A literature review'. *Studies in Higher Education*, 16(3): 319–32.

Hodges, L. (1991) 'Women set to win PhD stakes by 2001'. *Times Higher Education Supplement*, 25 January, 11.

Holmes, B. (1987) *The British PhD*. London: Committee of Vice-Chancellors and Principals of the Universities of the United Kingdom.

Hunter, J. H. (1880) 'The university question'. *Canada Educational Monthly*. January, 1–9.

Hutchins, R. M. and Adler, M. J. (1969) 'The idea of the university in the nineteenth century'. In Hutchins, R. M. and Adler, M. J. (eds) *Great Ideas Today*. New York: Encyclopedia Britannica.

Jacobsen, R. L. (1989) 'Educators and politicians from 100 countries urge campaign to make higher education more useful'. *Chronicle of Higher Education*, 25 January, A1, A37.

James, W. (1903) 'The PhD octopus'. *Harvard Monthly*, XXXVI(1), 7.

Jellama, W. W. (1986) 'The legacy of Rip Van Winkle'. In Steeples, D. W. (ed.) *Institutional Revival: Case Histories* (New Directions for Higher Education No. 54). San Francisco: Jossey-Bass.

Joll, J. (1970) In Tripp, R. T. (ed.) *The International Thesaurus of Quotations*. New York: Thomas Y. Crowell.

Kerr, C. (1971) *Less Time, More Options* (Conference Proceedings). Atlanta: Southern Regional Educational Board.

Kerr, C. (1975) 'Higher education in the United States in 1980 and 2000'. In Hostrop, R. W. (ed.) *Education Beyond Tomorrow*. Homewood: ETC Publications.

Kierkegaard, S. (1967) In Stevenson, B. (ed.) *Home Book of Quotations: Classical and Modern*. New York: Dood, Mead.

Kogan Page (1985) *A Comprehensive Guide to Educational, Technical, Professional and Academic Qualifications in Britain*. London: Kogan Page.

Kowalski, R. (1987) 'Slow PhDs'. *Times Higher Education Supplement*, 25 December, 10.

LaPidus, J. B. (1990) *Current Issues and Trends in Graduate Education* (Trevor N. S. Lennam Memorial Lecture on Graduate Education – 19 March, 1990). Calgary: University of Calgary.

Law, H. (1970) 'Strong medicine for scientists' plethora of PhDs'. *Canadian University and College*, 5(10), 29–31.

Leinster-Mackay, D. P. (1977) 'The idea of a university'. *Vestes*, 20(3–4), 28–33.

Levy, P. S. (1982) 'Surviving in a predominantly white male institution'. In Vartuli, S. (ed.) *The PhD Experience: A Woman's Point of View*. New York: Praeger Scientific.

Lockmiller, D. A. (1971) 'Degrees, academic'. In Deighton, L. C. (ed.) *The Encyclopedia of Education*. New York: Macmillan and Free Press. 25–32.

Louden, J. (1902) *The Universities in Relation to Research* (Presidential Address). Royal Society of Canada.

Lynton, E. A. and Elman, S. E. (1987) *New Priorities for the University*. San Francisco: Jossey-Bass.

MacGregor, K. (1991) 'Strict rules proposed for PhDs'. *Times Higher Education Supplement*, 30 August, 3.

Maclachlan, G. (1987) *On the Time Taken to Complete Graduate Research Degrees*. Ottawa: Canadian Association of Graduate Schools.

McLean, T. (1981) *The Black Female PhD*. Washington: University Press of America.

McLeish, J. (1992) *Number: From Ancient Civilizations to the Computer*. London: Flamingo.

McNeal, J., Hodysh H. H. and Konrad, A. G. (1981) *University Purposes* (History Committee Report, Senate Commission on University Purpose). Edmonton: University of Alberta.

Maslen, G. (1991a) 'Australia eases visa requirements for foreign teachers'. *Chronicle of Higher Education*, 3 April, A37.

Maslen, G. (1991b) 'Slow road to a PhD'. *Chronicle of Higher Education*, 30 August, 10.

Massué, J.-P. and Schinck, G. (1987) 'Doctoral training in Europe'. *Higher Education in Europe*, XII(4), 56–67.

Mayhew, L. B. (1977) 'Graduate and professional education'. In Knowles, A. S. (ed.) *The International Encyclopedia of Higher Education* (Volume 5). San Francisco: Jossey-Bass.

Mills, J. and Dombra, I. (1968) *University of Toronto Doctoral Theses 1897–1967*. Toronto: University of Toronto Press.

Mitchell, A. (1959) 'The university faculties'. In Price, A. G. (ed.) *The Humanities in Australia*. Sydney: Angus and Robertson.

Monaghan, P. (1989) 'Some fields are reassessing the value of the dissertation'. *Chronicle of Higher Education*, 29 March, A1, A16.

Monroe, P. (1911) *A Cyclopedia of Education* (Volume 2). New York: Macmillan.

Mooney, C. J. (1989a) 'Uncertainty is rampant as colleges begin to brace for faculty shortage expected to begin in 1990s'. *Chronicle of Higher Education*, 25 January, A14, A16, A17.

Mooney, C. J. (1989b) 'Professors are upbeat about profession but uneasy about students, standards'. *Chronicle of Higher Education*, 8 November, A1, A18–A21.

Moore, R. W. (1985) *Winning the PhD Game*. New York: Dodd Mead.

Moses, I. (1984) 'Supervision of higher degree students'. *Higher Education Research and Development*, 3(2), 153–65.

Neilson, W. A. and Gaffield, C. (1986) *Universities in Crisis: A Mediaeval Institution in the Twenty-first Century*. Halifax: Institute for Research on Public Policy.

Nichols, R. F. (1967) 'A reconsideration of the PhD'. *Graduate Journal*. 7(2), 325–35.

Nightingale, P. (1984) 'Examination of research and theses'. *Higher Education Research and Development*, 3(2), 137–50.

Noble, K. A. (1989) 'What a marketing survey of part-time students reveals about barriers to learning'. *Open Learning*, 4(2): 16–20.

Noble, K. A. (1992) *An International Prognostic Study, Based on an Acquisition Model, of the Degree Philosophiae Doctor* (PhD Thesis). Ottawa: University of Ottawa.

Nordvall, R. C. (1982) *The Process of Change in Higher Education* (AAHE-ERIC Higher Education Research Report No. 7). Washington: American Association for Higher Education.

Norris, W. (1989) 'Fast bucks for supermen in US patents scramble'. *Times Higher Education Supplement*, 13 January, 1.

Paludi, M. A. (1990) *Ivory Power: Sexual Harassment on Campus*. Albany: State University of New York.

Paulsen, F. (1908) *German Education*. London: T. Fisher Unwin.

Pelikan, J. (1983) *Scholarship and Its Survival: Questions on the Idea of Graduate Education*. Princeton: Carnegie Foundation for the Advancement of Teaching.

Perica, L. M. (1990) 'World organization for the future of higher education'. In Morrison, J. L. (ed.) *Global Change: Implications for the Future of Higher Education* (International Newsletter Number 13). Guildford: Society for Research into Higher Education, 20–2.

Phillips, E. M. and Pugh, D. S. (1987) *How to Get a PhD*. Milton Keynes: Open University Press.

Plowright, D. (1991) 'My PhD nightmare'. *Times Higher Education Supplement*, 6 December, 17.

Porter, J. (1970) *Post-Industrialism, Post-Nationalism, and Post-Secondary Education* (National Seminar Proceedings, June 1970). Ottawa: Institute of Public Administration of Canada.

Porter, J. *et al.* (1971) *Towards 2000*. Toronto: McClelland and Stewart.

Powles, M. (1988) *Know Your PhD Students and How to Help Them*. Melbourne: University of Melbourne.

Rait, R. S. (1912) *Life in the Mediaeval University*. Cambridge: Cambridge University Press.

Rashdall, H. (1895, 1936) *The Universities of Europe in the Middle Ages* (Volume I). Oxford: Clarendon Press.

Renouf, J. (1989) 'An alternative PhD'. *Area*, 21(1), 87–92.

Repo, M. (1970) *Who Needs the PhD?* Toronto: University of Toronto Graduate Students' Union.

Richards, H. (1991) 'Blacklisting remedy works for late theses'. *Times Higher Education Supplement*, 18 January, 5.

Ries, P. and Thurgood, D. H. (1993) *Summary Report 1991: Doctorate Recipients From United States Universities*. Washington, DC: National Academy Press.

Robbins, Lord *et al.* (1963) *Higher Education Report of the Robbins Royal Commission*. London: Her Majesty's Stationery Office.

Rosenhaupt, H. and Pinch, J. (1971) 'Doctoral degrees'. In Deighton, L. C. (ed.) *The Encyclopedia of Education*. New York: Macmillan and Free Press.

Rosovsky, H. (1990) *The University: An Owner's Manual*. London: W. W. Norton.

Ross, M. G. (1976) *The University: The Anatomy of Academe*. New York: McGraw-Hill.

Ross, P. N. (1975) 'The establishment of the PhD at Toronto'. In Katz, M. B. and Mattingly, P. H. (eds) *Education and Social Change*. New York: New York University Press.

Royce, J. R. (1964) *The Encapsulated Man*. New York: D. Van Nostrand.

Rudd, E. (1985) *A New Look at Postgraduate Failure*. Guildford: The Society for Research into Higher Education.

Rudd, E. and Simpson, R. (1975) *The Highest Education*. London: Routledge and Kegan Paul.

Professor The Earl Russell (1988) Letter to the editor. *Times Higher Education Supplement*, 26 February, p. 12.

Salk, J. (1992) *Ulrich's International Periodical Directory* (1992–3). New York: R. R. Bowker.

Salmon, P. (1992) *Achieving a PhD: Ten Students' Experience*. Stoke-on-Trent: Trentham Books.

Sartain, W. J. (1955) 'The university and research'. *Cambridge Review*, 30 April, 482, 483, 485.

Schachner, N. (1962) *The Mediaeval Universities*. New York: A. S. Barnes.

Scott, P. (1984) *The Crisis of the University*. London: Croom Helm.

Scott, P. (1989) 'Sitting out the quickstep'. *Times Higher Education Supplement*, 14 July, 7.

Sekhon, J. G. (1989) 'PhD education and Australia's industrial future'. *Higher Education Research and Development*, 8(2), 191–215.

Seymour, D. T. (1987) 'Out on a limb: Why administrators must take risks'. *Educational Record*, 68(2), 36–40.

Seymour, D. T. (1988) *Developing Academic Programs: The Climate for Innovation* (ASHE-ERIC Higher Education Report Number 3). Washington: Association for the Study of Higher Education.

Shores, L. (1961) *Collier's Encyclopedia* (Volume 1). New York: Crowell-Collier.

Simpson, R. (1983) *How the PhD Came to Britain*. Guildford: Society for Research into Higher Education.

Slosson, E. E. (1910) *Great American Universities*. New York: Macmillan.

Smith, C. R. (1988) In Simpson, J. B. (ed.) *Simpson's Contemporary Quotations*. Boston, Houghton Mifflin.

Smith, D. M. and Saunders, M. R. (1991) *Others Routes: Part-Time Higher Education Policy*. Milton Keynes: Open University Press.

Smith, K. A. (1989) Correspondence from University Archivist. University of Sydney, 5 September.

Smith, P. (1990) *Killing the Spirit: Higher Education in America*. New York: Penguin Books.

Smith, S. L. *et al*. (1991) *Report*. Ottawa: Association of Universities and Colleges of Canada.

Solomon, R. and Solomon J. (1993) *Up the University: Re-Creating Higher Education in America*. New York: Addison-Wesley.

Spurr, S. H. (1970) *Academic Degree Structures*. New York: McGraw-Hill.

Squair, J. (1904) 'Lessons from lost opportunities'. *University of Toronto Monthly*, October, 10.

Sternberg, D. J. (1981) *How to Complete and Survive a Doctoral Dissertation*. New York: St. Martin's Press.

Stine, S. B. (1989) 'The business of the business'. *Policy Perspectives*, 1(3), 1–7.

Stone, L. (1990) Communication from Library Information Services, University of Auckland, 9 January.

Storr, R. F. (1973) *The Beginning of the Future*. New York: McGraw-Hill.

Stranks, D. R. (1984) 'PhD education in the nineties'. *Higher Education Research and Development*, 3(2), 167–75.

Surridge, O. (1989) 'New Yorker calls for thesis to be dropped from PhDs'. *Times Higher Education Supplement*, 20 January, 2.

Swann, M. (1968) *The Flow Into Employment of Scientists, Engineers and Technologists*. London: Her Majesty's Stationery Office.

Swinnerton-Dyer, P. *et al*. (1982) *Report of the Working Party on Postgraduate Education*. London: Her Majesty's Stationery Office.

Sykes, C. J. (1988) *ProfScam: Professors and the Demise of Higher Education*. Washington: Regnery Gateway.

Symons, T. H. and Page, J. E. (1984) *Some Questions of Balance* (Volume 3). Ottawa: Association of Universities and Colleges of Canada.

Thompson, I. and Roberts, A. (1985) *The Road Retaken: Women Re-enter the Academy*. New York: Modern Language Association.

Thwing, C. F. (1928) *The American and the German University*. New York: Macmillan.

Tight, M. (1990) *Higher Education: A Part-Time Perspective*. Milton Keynes: SRHE and Open University Press.

Tight, M. (1993) Personal communication with Senior Lecturer, University of Warwick, 18 February.

Times Higher Education Supplement. (1991) 'Commercial campus'. 26 June, 32.

Times Higher Education Supplement. (1993) 'Review of journals is long overdue'. 26 February, 14.

Turner, A. J. (1988) 'Structure and aims of postgraduate education policy in the UK and the US'. *Biochemical Education*, 16: 136–9.

Vandament, W. E. (1988) 'Those who would reform undergraduate education must recognize the realities of academic governance'. *Chronicle of Higher Education*, 30 November, A52.

Vartuli, S. (1982) *The PhD Experience: A Woman's Point of View*. New York: Praeger Scientific.

Veysey, L. R. (1965) *The Emergence of the American University*. Chicago: University of Chicago Press.

Waller, G. (1992) Correspondence from Superintendent, Manuscripts Reading Room, University of Cambridge Library, 16 March.

Walters, E. (1965) 'The rise of graduate education'. In Walters E. (ed.) *Graduate Education Today*. Washington: American Council on Education. 1–29.

Welford, J. (1991) 'When a PhD is less than appealing'. *Times Higher Education Supplement*, 6 September, 18.

Weston, J. (1988a) 'First joint PhD program pioneers way for others'. *University Affairs*, February, 2, 3.

Weston, J. (1988b) 'Can curriculum be revamped?'. *University Affairs*, November, 40.

Whitaker, J. (1992) *Books in Print 1992*. London: J. Whitaker and Sons.

Whitney, J. (1987) 'Readers respond on the role of the university professor'. *In Touch*, 4(3), 2.

Wilcox, W. (1975) 'The university in the United States of America'. In Stephens, M. D. and Roderick, G. W. (eds) *Universities for a Changing World*. London: David and Charles.

Williams, E. (1988) 'PhD overhaul to compromise on taught courses'. *Times Higher Education Supplement*, 8 April, 1.

Winfield, G. (1987) 'Doctors fighting with an octopus'. *Times Higher Education Supplement*, 27 March, 15.

Winfield, G. *et al.* (1987) *The Social Science PhD: The ESRC Enquiry of Submission Rates* (Report). London: ESRC.

Wolfe, D. and Kidd, C. V. (1971) 'The future market for PhDs'. *Science*, 173, 783–93.

Wright, J. (1991) 'Left to their own devices'. *Times Higher Education Supplement*, 6 December, 16, 17.

Wright, J. and Lodwick, R. (1989) 'The process of the PhD: A study of the first year of doctoral study'. *Research Papers in Education*, 4(1), 22–56.

Xerox University Microfilms (1973) *Comprehensive Dissertation Index 1861–1972*. Ann Arbor: Xerox Corporation.

Young, A. H. (1903) 'The University of Oxford and colonial graduates'. *The Times*, 19 September, 7.

Young, K., Fogarty, M. P. and McRae, S. (1987) *The Management of Doctoral Studies in the Social Sciences*, London: Policy Studies Institute.

Ziolkowski, T. (1990) 'The PhD squid'. *American Scholar*, 59(2), 177–95.

Zur-Muehlen, M. von. (1978) 'The PhD dilemma in Canada revisited'. *Canadian Journal of Higher Education*, VIII(2), 49–92.

Zur-Muehlen, M. von. (1987) 'A faculty supply crisis in the 1990s seems unlikely'. *University Affairs*, March 17.

Index

The Society for Research into Higher Education

The Society for Research into Higher Education exists to stimulate and co-ordinate research into all aspects of higher education. It aims to improve the quality of higher education through the encouragement of debate and publication on issues of policy, on the organization and management of higher education institutions, and on the curriculum and teaching methods.

The Society's income is derived from subscriptions, sales of its books and journals, conference fees and grants. It receives no subsidies, and is wholly independent. Its individual members include teachers, researchers, managers and students. Its corporate members are institutions of higher education, research institutes, professional, industrial and governmental bodies. Members are not only from the UK, but from elsewhere in Europe, from America, Canada and Australasia, and it regards its international work as amongst its most important activities.

Under the imprint *SRHE & Open University Press*, the Society is a specialist publisher of research, having some 45 titles in print. The Editorial Board of the Society's Imprint seeks authoritative research or study in the above fields. It offers competitive royalties, a highly recognizable format in both hardback and paperback and the world-wide reputation of the Open University Press.

The Society also publishes *Studies in Higher Education* (three times a year), which is mainly concerned with academic issues, *Higher Education Quarterly* (formerly *Universities Quarterly*), mainly concerned with policy issues, *Research into Higher Education Abstracts* (three times a year), and *SRHE News* (four times a year).

The Society holds a major annual conference in December, jointly with an institution of higher education. In 1991, the topic was 'Research and Higher Education in Europe', with the University of Leicester. In 1992, it was 'Learning to Effect' with the Nottingham Trent University and in 1993, 'Governments and the Higher Education Curriculum' at the University of Sussex in Brighton. Future conferences include in 1994, 'The Student Experience' at the University of York.

The Society's committees, study groups and branches are run by the members. The groups at present include:

Teacher Education Study Group
Continuing Education Group
Staff Development Group
Excellence in Teaching and Learning

Benefits to members

Individual

Individual members receive:

- *SRHE News*, the Society's publications list, conference details and other material included in mailings.
- Greatly reduced rates for *Studies in Higher Education* and *Higher Education Quarterly*.
- A 35% discount on all Open University Press & SRHE publications.
- Free copies of the Precedings – commissioned papers on the theme of the Annual Conference.
- Free copies of *Research into Higher Education Abstracts*.
- Reduced rates for conferences.
- Extensive contacts and scope for facilitating initiatives.
- Reduced reciprocal memberships.

Corporate

Corporate members receive:

- All benefits of individual members, plus
- Free copies of *Studies in Higher Education*.
- Unlimited copies of the Society's publications at reduced rates.
- Special rates for its members e.g. to the Annual Conference.

Membership details: SRHE, 344–354 Gray's Inn Road, London, WC1X 8BP, UK. Tel: 071 837 7880
Catalogue: SRHE & Open University Press, Celtic Court, 22 Ballmoor, Buckingham MK18 1XW. Tel: (0280) 823388